A
Sister Carrie

PORTFOLIO

<u>Sister Carrie</u>.
C H A P T E R   I .   *About 150,000 words*

The *magnet attracting: a waif amid forces.*

When Caroline Meeber boarded the afternoon train for Chicago, her total outfit consisted of a small trunk, ~~which was checked in the baggage car~~, a cheap imitation alligator skin satchel, ~~holding some minor details of the toilet~~, a small lunch in a paper box and a yellow leather snap purse, containing her ticket, a scrap of paper with her sister's address in Van Buren Street, and four dollars in money.   It was in August, 1889.   She was eighteen years of age, bright, timid ~~and~~ full of *the* illusions *of* ignorance and youth.   Whatever touch of regret at parting characterized her thoughts, it was certainly not for advantages now being given up.   A gush of tears at her mother's farewell kiss, a touch in the throat when the cars clacked by the flour mill where her father worked by the day, a pathetic sigh as the familiar green environs of the village passed in review, and the threads which bound her so lightly to girlhood and home were irretrievably broken.

To be sure, ~~she was not conscious of any of this.   Any change, however great, might be remedied.~~   There was always the next station where one might descend and return.   There was the great city bound more closely by these very trains which came up daily. Columbia City was not so very far away, even once she was in Chicago. What, pray, is a few hours - a *few* hundred miles?   ~~And then her sister was there.~~   She looked at the little slip bearing ~~the latter's~~ *her sister's* address and wondered.   She gazed at the green landscape, now passing in swift review, until her swifter thoughts replaced its impression with vague conjectures of what Chicago might be, ~~like.   Since infancy her ears had been full of its fame.   Ever the family had thought of~~

A
Sister Carrie
PORTFOLIO

JAMES L. W. WEST III

Published for the Bibliographical Society
of the University of Virginia
by the University Press of Virginia
Charlottesville

Published for the Bibliographical Society
of the University of Virginia
by the University Press of Virginia
Charlottesville
THE UNIVERSITY PRESS OF VIRGINIA
Copyright © 1985 by the Rector and Visitors
of the University of Virginia

First published 1985

Library of Congress Cataloging in Publication Data

West, James L. W. III
    A Sister Carrie portfolio.

    1. Dreiser, Theodore, 1871-1945. Sister Carrie.
2. Dreiser, Theodore, 1871-1945—Manuscripts—Facsimiles.
I. University of Virginia. Bibliographical Society.
II. Title.
PS3507.R55S597 1985   813'.52   85-5370
ISBN 0-8139-1067-6

The preparation of this volume was supported
in part by a grant from the American Council
of Learned Societies.

Frontis.: The first page of the typescript setting copy of *Sister Carrie*.

iv

Preface

This book is a pictorial history of the making of Theodore Dreiser's first novel, *Sister Carrie*. The images presented here are complementary to the full-dress scholarly edition of *Sister Carrie* published in the spring of 1981 by University of Pennsylvania Press. Based on Dreiser's surviving manuscript at the New York Public Library and on the typescript setting copy of the novel at the University of Pennsylvania, this 1981 edition presented a text of *Sister Carrie* significantly different from the first-edition version published by Doubleday, Page & Co. in November 1900.*

A six-year study of the surviving evidence by the editors of the 1981 edition revealed that Dreiser's narrative had been censored and cut in 1900, before publication, in order to tone down its blunt treatment of sex and soften its harsh, deterministic philosophy. Dreiser had also rewritten his original ending in order to make it more equivocal, more acceptable to genteel readers of his day. Throughout the composition of the novel Dreiser had worked closely with his wife, Sara (or "Jug," as she was called), and his friend Arthur Henry. These two made or suggested most of the changes in the manuscript and typescript. Jug and Henry meant well, but the cumulative effect of their efforts was to change *Sister Carrie*, to damage it as a literary work.

In the new *Sister Carrie*, cut and censored passages are reinstated, misguided corrections are reversed, stylistic tinkerings are rejected, and the original ending is restored. Mild profanity, removed before publication at the insistence of Doubleday, Page & Co., is reintroduced in the text. And names of real public figures, businesses, theaters, actors, writers, and books—also changed at the publisher's insistence—are restored. The resulting novel is significantly different from the book published in 1900; this new *Sister Carrie* is a changed work of art, stronger and more fully realized than the novel Americans read for eighty years.

The 1981 edition contains historical and textual introductions, extensive annotations, maps, tables, and appendices. It is a scholar's edition, with the kinds of commentary and apparatus one expects to find in such an edition. It also contains eight illustrations, but only two of these are documentary facsimiles—small reproductions of the first page of the manuscript and the first page of the typescript. The reader, as a result, misses the visual aspect of the *Sister Carrie* project. A great deal of evidence bearing on the early history of the novel survives, and much of it is fascinating to look at. On the leaves of the manuscript, one can see Jug censoring references to sex and Henry "improving" Dreiser's prose. In the typescript one can see Frank Doubleday's pen calling attention to profane words, and one can observe Dreiser's reluctant compliance with the insistent blue pencil of the Doubleday, Page & Co. editor. One can even see the printer's galley marks, spike holes, and inky fingerprints. Such evidence is described at various points in the 1981 edition, but descriptions are unsatisfactory substitutes for seeing the actual documents, and few readers can travel to New York and Philadelphia to do so.

This portfolio supplies the visual dimension missing from the 1981 edition of *Sister Carrie*. It provides an account, in facsimiles and photographs, of the making of Dreiser's novel. This volume is directed toward scholars, students, and especially toward teachers of the new text. Reproduced here are the most interesting leaves from the original manuscript and typescript, together with facsimiles of other documents—correspondence, contracts, title pages, and miscellaneous items. This portfolio tells, with pictures and words, the intriguing story of the composition and publication of *Sister Carrie*.

This volume is also meant to demonstrate for the reader some of the pleasures of manuscript study. The thrill of holding the document in hand is important, and there is also the challenge of the detective work, the anticipation of the puzzle that must be solved, the pursuit of the evidence that must be assembled. This evidence is here arranged to tell a story; the pictures and captions show the progress of *Sister Carrie* from manuscript to typescript to first edition. The facsimiles supply visual images, the commentary relates these images one to another, and the captions supply detail.

Internal documentation is minimal. There are no footnotes in the body of the book. References to the manuscript are by chapter and leaf number: "MS.VII.17," for example, stands for leaf 17 in chapter VII of the manuscript. References to the typescript are by leaf number only (e.g., "TS.144"), since the typescript is foliated consecutively.

My debt to the American Council of Learned Societies is recorded on the copyright page of this volume. For permission to reproduce leaves from the manuscript I thank the Rare Books and Manuscript Division, New York Public Library, Astor, Lenox and Tilden Foundations; for permission to facsimile leaves from the typescript and to reproduce other documents from the Dreiser Papers I thank the Charles Patterson Van Pelt Library, University of Pennsylvania. For advice and encouragement I am grateful to the genial Mr. John D. Stinson, Assistant Curator of Manuscripts, New York Public Library, and to my friend Dr. Neda M. Westlake, recently retired Curator of Rare Books at the University of Pennsylvania. Photographic assistance was rendered by Lee Ann Droud and by Bernard Baker and his staff at the LRC Photo Lab, Virginia Polytechnic Institute. For other considerations I wish to mention Vera Dreiser, Anita Malebranche, Dorothy McCombs, Joseph McElrath, Donald T. Oakes, and Daniel Traister. I should also like to thank the administrators and staff of the National Humanities Center, where the final revision of this study was carried out.

*Sister Carrie, historical editors, John C. Berkey and Alice M. Winters; textual editor, James L. W. West III; general editor, Neda M. Westlake (Philadelphia: Univ. of Pennsylvania Press, 1981). A classroom edition is published by the Penguin American Library. For major reviews and reactions, see Alfred Kazin, *New York Review of Books*, 19 Feb. 1981, pp. 12–14; Herbert Mitgang, *New York Times*, 17 Apr. 1981, pp. 1, 16A; Justin Kaplan, *New York Times Book Review*, 31 May 1981, pp. 13 ff; Richard Lingeman, *Nation*, 11–18 July 1981, pp. 53–57; Richard H. Brodhead, *Yale Review*, 71 (Summer 1982), 597–600; Donald Pizer, *American Literature*, 53 (Jan. 1982), 731–37; Hershel Parker, *Resources for American Literary Study*, 11 (Autumn 1981), 332–36; Richard W. Dowell, *Dreiser Newsletter*, 12 (Spring 1981), 1–8; Ron Hansen, *Michigan Quarterly Review*, 22 (Fall 1983), 661–64; Joseph K. Davis, *Sewanee Review*, 91 (Summer 1983), 454–57.

Dreiser in 1893, about a year before meeting Arthur Henry.

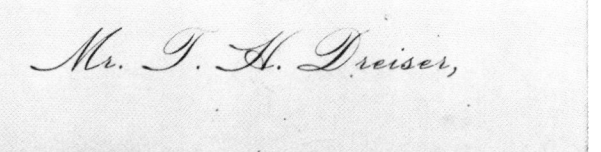

Dreiser's card from his days as a cub reporter for the *St. Louis Republic*.

Arthur Henry, a talkative and charming man, had literary ambitions.

Preliminaries

The story of *Sister Carrie* began in March 1894 when Theodore Dreiser met Arthur Henry in Toledo, Ohio. Dreiser, a wandering newspaperman, had been writing for the *Daily Globe* in Chicago and for the *Globe-Democrat* and the *Republic* in St. Louis. Henry, city editor of the *Toledo Blade*, gave Dreiser temporary employment covering a streetcar strike. The two struck up a close friendship and kept in contact after Dreiser moved on to Cleveland and then to Buffalo.

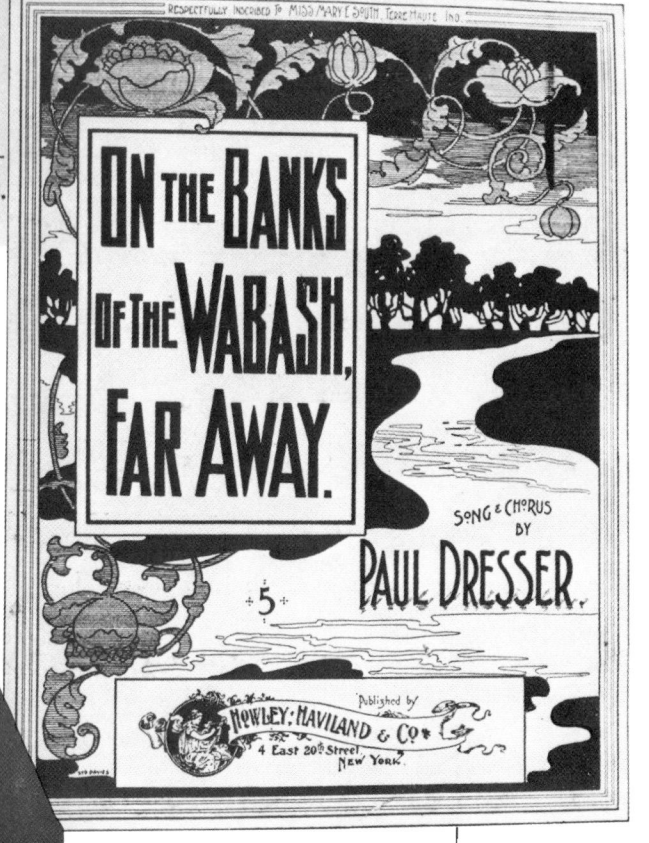

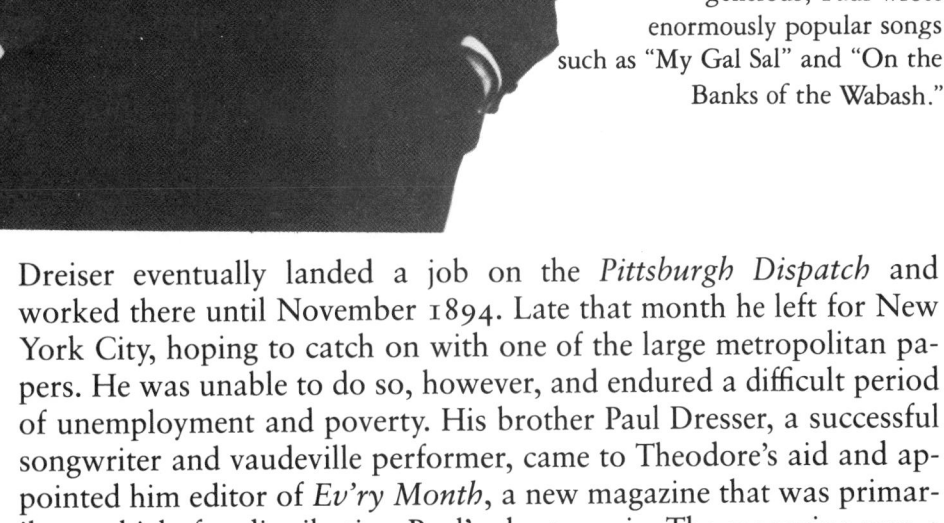

Paul Dresser, at the peak of his career. Sentimental and generous, Paul wrote enormously popular songs such as "My Gal Sal" and "On the Banks of the Wabash."

Dreiser eventually landed a job on the *Pittsburgh Dispatch* and worked there until November 1894. Late that month he left for New York City, hoping to catch on with one of the large metropolitan papers. He was unable to do so, however, and endured a difficult period of unemployment and poverty. His brother Paul Dresser, a successful songwriter and vaudeville performer, came to Theodore's aid and appointed him editor of *Ev'ry Month*, a new magazine that was primarily a vehicle for distributing Paul's sheet music. The magazine was a success and gave Dreiser a start on the New York literary scene.

2

Cover of the December 1896 issue of *Ev'ry Month*. In addition to Paul's sheet music, the magazine printed other materials: fiction, poetry, advice to women, and "philosophical" columns by Dreiser (who published much work here under pseudonyms).

Dreiser and Jug early in their marriage. She had been
a schoolteacher and was well-educated for her time.
(Photo courtesy of Vera Dreiser.)

In 1897 Dreiser left *Ev'ry Month* and became a free-lance writer spe-
cializing in factual articles and interviews. By December 1898 he was
successful enough to marry Sara Osborne White (whom everyone
called "Jug"), and the two settled in a New York flat.

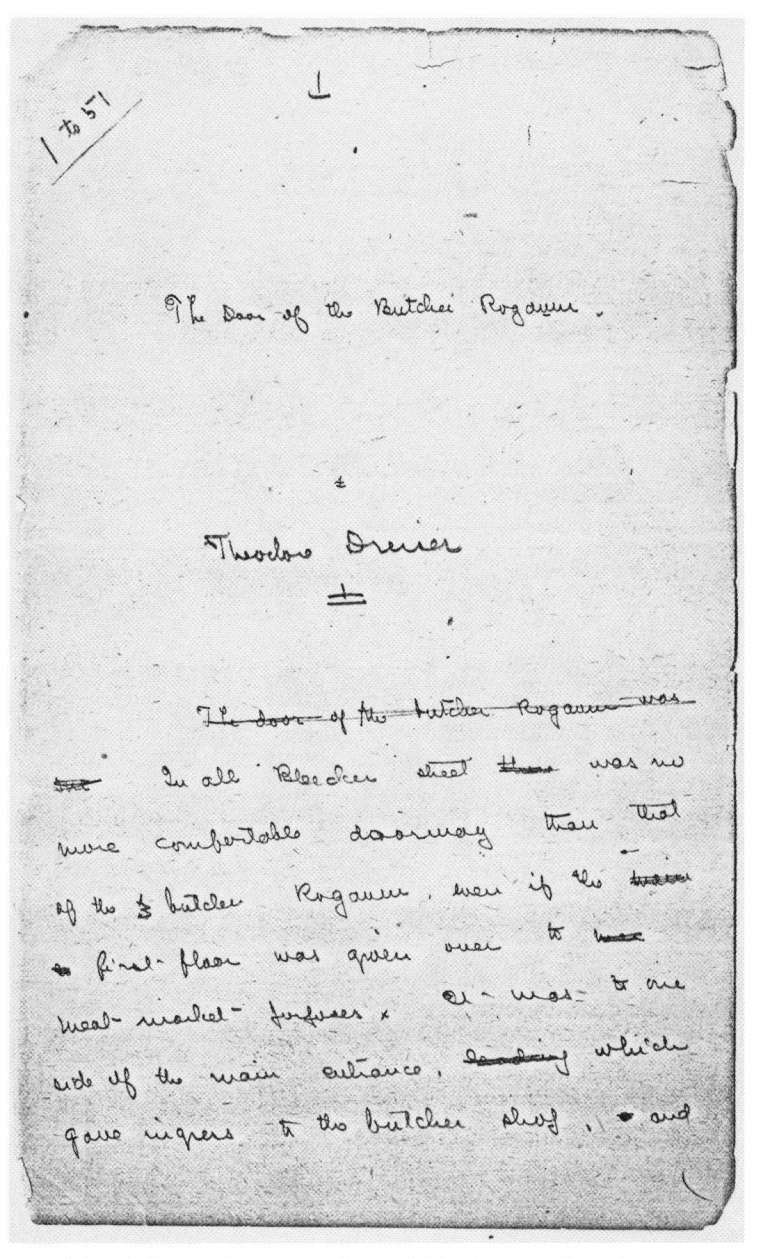

First page of the holograph manuscript of "The Door of the Butcher Rogaum," a story about German-Americans in New York City.

During the summer of 1899 Dreiser and Jug visited Arthur Henry and his wife in Maumee, Ohio. While there Dreiser—egged on by Henry—decided to try his hand at fiction. He produced four short stories: "When the Old Century Was New," "The Shining Slave Makers," "Nigger Jeff," and "The Door of the Butcher Rogaum." All four were eventually placed with magazines, and Dreiser's career as a writer of fiction was under way.

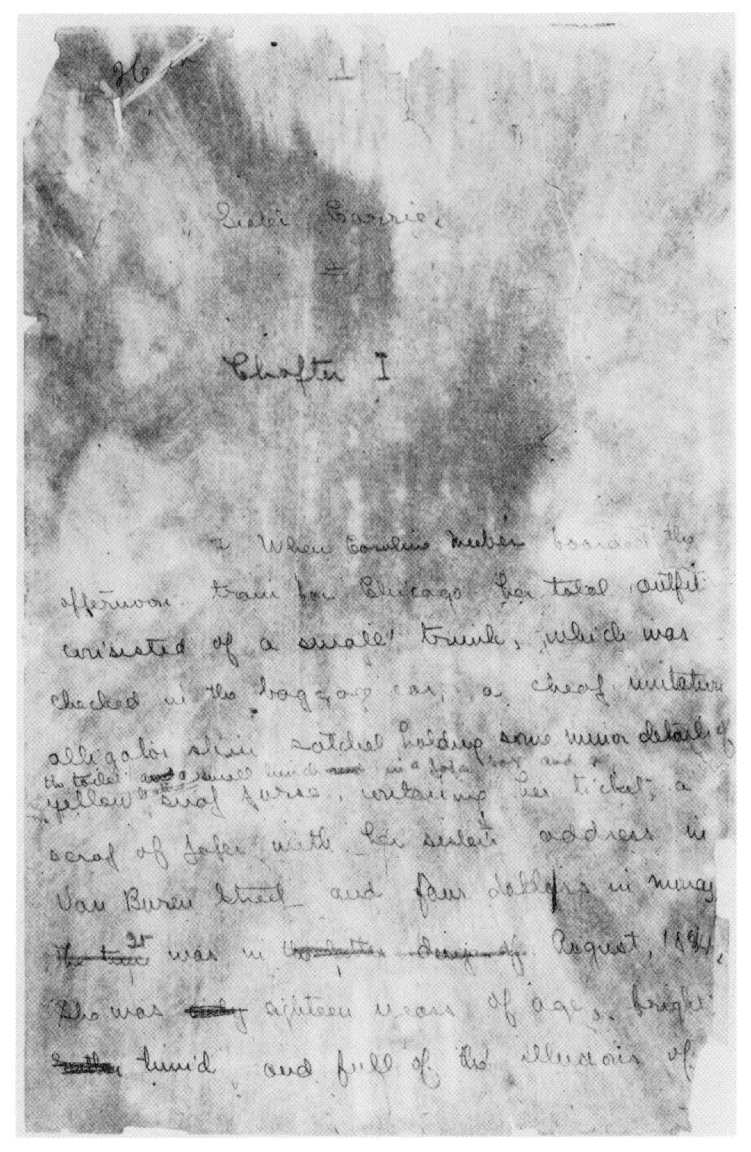

MS.I.1: The first leaf of the *Sister Carrie* manuscript. Because this leaf rested on top of the manuscript for many years, it is heavily discolored.

Henry was writing a novel called *A Princess of Arcady*, and he wanted Dreiser to begin a novel so they could compose their books together. Dreiser held off for a time but eventually gave in to Henry's prodding. He took a newspaper "second sheet" and penciled the words *Sister Carrie* at the top. Years later he would tell interviewers and biographers that, when he began his novel, he had no clear idea what it would contain, what direction it would take. Modern scholars have discounted this story, but there remains an exciting, mystical quality about the first leaf of the manuscript of *Sister Carrie*.

Emma Dreiser, the author's sister, who fled to Canada from Chicago with her married lover.

Composition of the Manuscript

Dreiser wanted to write a realistic novel. He based his plot loosely on an adulterous escapade involving his sister Emma, and he drew background from his experiences as a reporter and journalist in Chicago and New York. He filled the manuscript with names of real persons like pugilist John L. Sullivan and actress Lillian Russell, and he mentioned actual places like the Potter Palmer mansion in Chicago and the Waldorf Astoria in New York.

Lillian Russell, famous actress
and singer, who stars
in the first professional
production Carrie appears in.
Carrie is a lowly member
of the chorus line.

John L. Sullivan, last bare-knuckle
heavyweight champion. In
Sister Carrie Sullivan is a customer
at Hannah and Hogg's,
the "resort" managed by
Hurstwood. We see him there at
the bar, "surrounded by a company
of loudly-dressed sports."

Jefferson Jones, a famous actor who is mentioned
several times in *Sister Carrie*. Jones appears here in
costume as Rip Van Winkle, his most famous role.

The Potter Palmer mansion in Chicago. Drouet
points out this residence to Carrie during one of their
buggy rides.

The Waldorf-Astoria as it
looked in the early 1890s.
At the end of the novel, Carrie
and her companion Lola live in
"comfortable chambers" here.

MS.I.10: At this point Dreiser began to splice in the Ade passage. The arrow shows the spot at which he cut and glued the manuscript leaves.

Dreiser also did a bit of plagiarizing. He was so taken by a sketch of George Ade's called "The Fable of the Two Violin Players and the Willing Performer" that he lifted a description of a "masher" from the piece and spliced it into the first chapter of his manuscript.

Family, and had been schooled in the Proprieties, and it was not to be supposed that she would crave the Society of slangy old Gus, who had an abounding Nerve, and furthermore was as Fresh as the Mountain Air.

He was the Kind of Fellow who would see a Girl twice, and then, upon meeting her the Third Time, he would go up and straighten her Cravat for her, and call her by her First Name.

Put him into a Strange Company —en route to a Picnic—and by the time the Baskets were unpacked he would have a Blonde all to himself, and she would have traded her Fan for his College Pin.

If a Fair-Looker on the Street happened to glance at him Hard he would run up and seize her by the Hand, and

185

convince her that they had Met. And he always Got Away with it, too.

In a Department Store, while waiting for the Cash Boy to come back with the Change, he would find out the Girl's Name, her Favorite Flower, and where a Letter would reach her.

Upon entering a Parlor Car at St. Paul he would select a Chair next to the Most Promising One in Sight, and ask her if she cared to have the Shade lowered.

Before the Train cleared the Yards he would have the Porter bringing a Foot-Stool for the Lady.

At Hastings he would be asking her if she wanted Something to Read.

At Red Wing he would be telling her that she resembled Maxine Elliott, and showing her his Watch, left to him by his Grandfather, a Prominent Virginian.

186

Pages 185 and 186 from Ade's humorous sketch as it appeared in *Fables in Slang* (1899). Dreiser probably first saw the sketch in the *Chicago Record* for 7 October 1899. The passages he borrowed are indicated in these facsimiles.

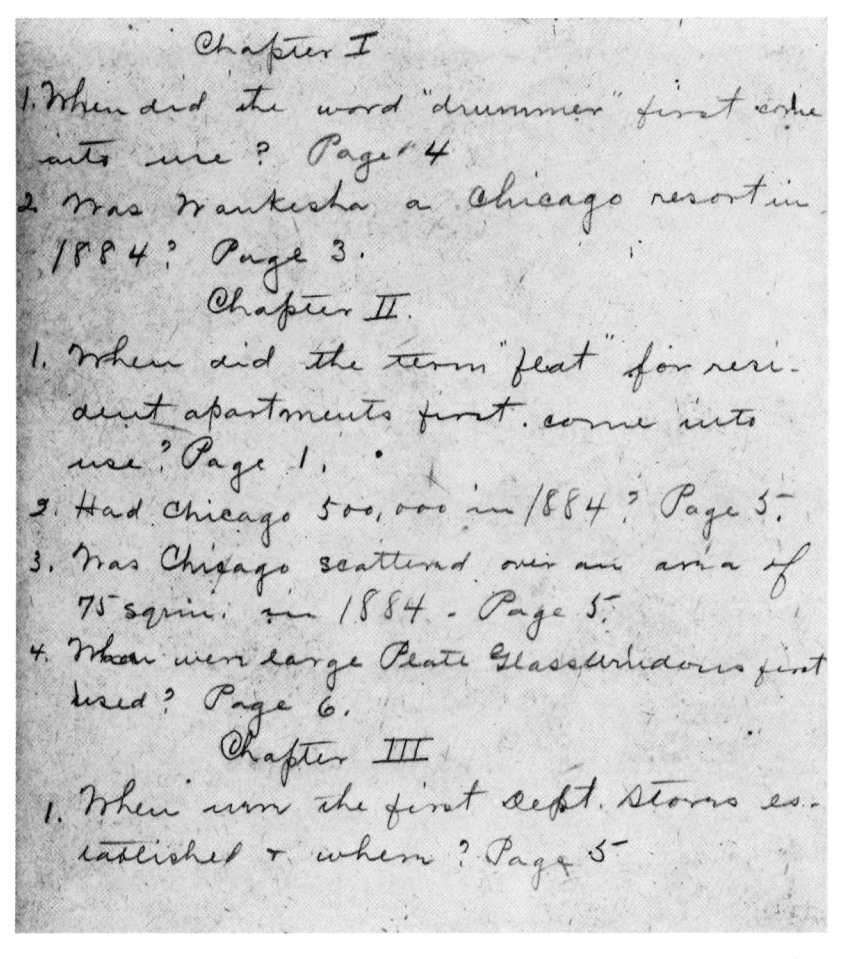

Jug's questions are answered in the historical notes on pp. 558–59 of the
Pennsylvania edition.

He finished three chapters and gave them to Jug for her reaction. She
apparently liked the story but was concerned about the historical ac-
curacy of certain words and passages. She made a list of queries for
her husband.

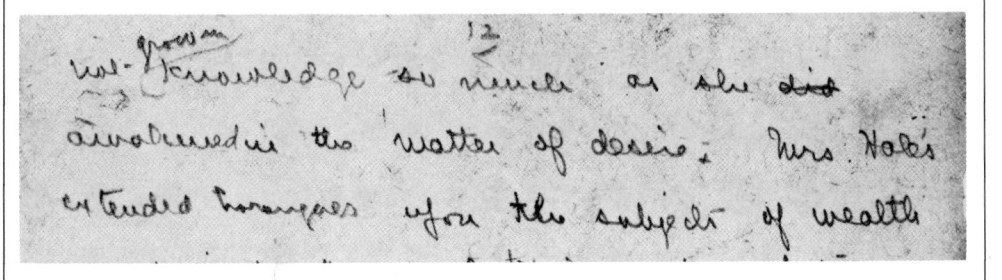

Detail from MS. VIII. 9 showing grammatical corrections in Jug's hand.

Detail from MS. XIII. 12: Here Henry tinkers with Dreiser's wording and style.

Jug made some revisions in what Dreiser had written, as did Henry. Dreiser was used to working with copy editors and rewrite men from his newspaper days, and he seems not to have minded this kind of "help." Jug, attentive and careful, corrected many mechanical errors but made few major revisions. Henry, by contrast, read less carefully and was inclined to make more significant changes.

MS.IX.17, the last page of chapter IX in the manuscript. Dreiser was unable to push past this point for two months.

Dreiser finished nine chapters and then stalled. He had introduced Carrie, Drouet, and Hurstwood into the narrative, but he could not decide how to develop the relationship between Carrie and Hurstwood. Dreiser put the novel down for two months, apparently believing he would never return to it. Encouraged by Henry, however, Dreiser picked the manuscript back up in mid-December 1899 and pushed through the problem spot, writing the chapters in which Hurstwood attempts to take Carrie from Drouet.

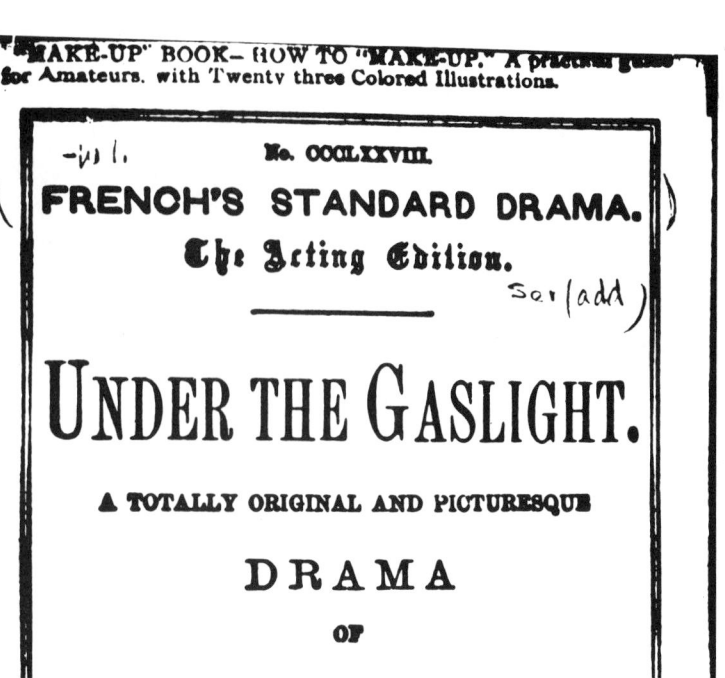

No. CCCLXXVIII.

FRENCH'S STANDARD DRAMA.

The Acting Edition.

Ser (add)

UNDER THE GASLIGHT.

A TOTALLY ORIGINAL AND PICTURESQUE

DRAMA

OF

LIFE AND LOVE IN THESE TIMES,

IN FIVE ACTS,

BY AUGUSTIN DALY,

Author of "Leah, the Forsaken;" "Griffith Gaunt," &c., &c.

AUTHOR'S EDITION.

FROM
WALTER H. BAKER & CO

H, LTD.
SA... ...N ST.
24 W... ...W. C.

MAKE-UP BOX.

Containing Rouge, Pearl Powder, Whiting, Mongolian, Ruddy Rouge, Violet Powder Box and Puff, Chrome, Blue, Burnt Cork, Pencils for the eyelids, Spirit Gum, India Ink, Camel Hair Brushes, Hare's Foot, Wool, Craped Hair, Cold Cream, Joining Paste, Miniature Puffs, Scissors and Looking Glass : packed neatly in Strong Fancy Card-board Boxes, $1.00 ; Elegant Tin Cases, $5.00
THE ABOVE ARTICLES TO BE HAD SEPARATELY For Prices, see Catalogue

NO PLAYS EXCHANGED.

Dreiser used
this edition of
Under the Gaslight
in composing
Sister Carrie.

In this part of the novel Carrie appears on stage in an amateur production sponsored by Drouet's chapter of the Elks Club. Dreiser cast her in Augustin Daly's melodrama *Under the Gaslight*, and for realism he incorporated actual dialogue and stage directions from the Samuel French "Author's Edition" of the play into his narrative.

Sue Earlie. What can it mean?

Mrs. Van D. It means that the rumors of ten years ago are proven. It was then suspected that the girl whom Mrs. COURTLAND brought every year from some unnamed place in the country, and introduced to everybody as her niece, was an impostor, which that foolish woman, in a freak of generosity, was thrusting upon society. The rumors died out for want of proof—and before LAURA's beauty and dignity—but now they are confirmed. She is some beggar's child.

Sue Earlie. What do you think we ought to do? (TRAFFORD *surrenders* PEARL *to* DEMILT, *and comes down.*)

Mrs. Van D. Tell it—tell it everywhere, of course. The best blood of New York is insulted by the girl's presence. (TRAFFORD *coming down.*)

Ray. (R. H.) What have you three girls got your heads together for? Some conspiracy, I know.

Mrs. Van D. (*To ladies.*) Go girls—tell it everywhere.

Ray. (*As the ladies distribute themselves about the groups.*) What is it all about? Your face is like a portrait of mystery.

Mrs. Van D. (*Showing letter.*) Look at this, and tell me what it means.

Ray. (*Quickly*) Where did you get this?

Mrs. Van D. It is you who must answer—and Society that will question. So LAURA is not a COURTLAND?

Ray. (*Overcome.*) You know, then.

Mrs. Van D. Everything; and will you marry this creature? You cannot. Society will not permit your sacrifice.

Detail from page 13 of the Samuel French edition of *Under the Gaslight.*

it, read & and published the information then and there.

"What can it mean?" questions one of her hearers.

"It means", says this character, "that the rumors of ten years ago are proven. It was then suspected that the girl whom Mrs. Courtland brought every year from some unnamed place in the country, and introduced to everybody as her niece, was an impostor, which that foolish woman, in a freak of generosity, was thrusting upon society. The rumors died out for want of proof—and before Laura's beauty and dignity—but now they are confirmed. She is some beggar's child.

"What do you think we ought to do," asks one.

"Tell it—tell it everywhere, of course.

MS. XVII. 28, on which Dreiser copied text from the page above.

17

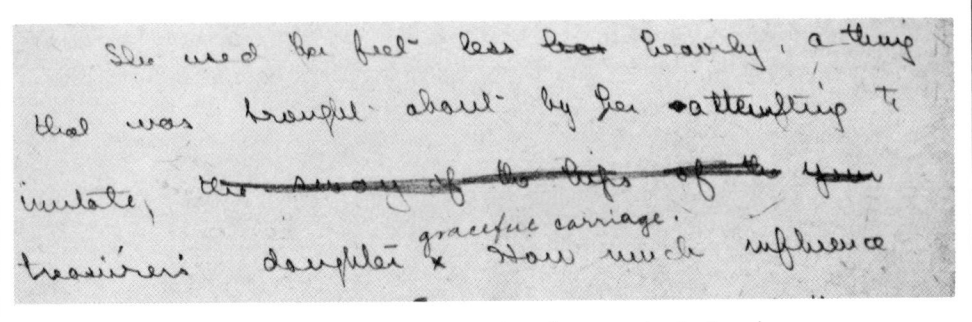

Detail from MS.XI.20, on which Jug revises "suggestive" phrasing.

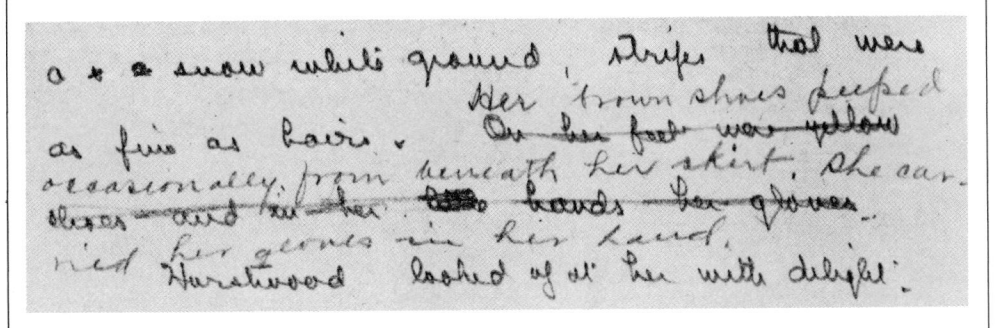

Detail from MS.XVI.24: Here Jug makes a stylistic revision.

Jug had by now become bolder in her revising. She had also begun to tone down some of the profanity and sex in the novel. She was likely motivated in part by her own moral standards, which were conservative, but she must also have believed that no publisher of the day would print the words and passages she was censoring.

MS.XVI.21: References to Carrie's "corsets" and
"body" are removed by Jug.

When he had finished it he stood holding
it in his hands. The audacity of the
thing took his breath. It roused his ire
also — the deepest element of revolt in
him. His first impulse was to write
but [to] fewer words in reply. "Go to the
devil"; but he compromised by telling the boy
that there would be no reply. Then he
sat down in his chair and gazed without
seeing, contemplating the result of his work.
What would she do after that. The confounded
wretch! was she going to try to bull-doze
him into submission. He would go up
there and have it out with her, that's
what he would do. She was carrying things
with too high a hand. No, by God, he
wouldn't be ordered like that. She could
do what she damn pleased. He would let
her take care of herself. She could wait
now until he got good and ready. There

MS. XXIV. 9: Here Jug supplies the word *wretch* where Dreiser apparently
wanted to use *bitch*.

Anna Mallon.

Preparation of the Typescript

Dreiser had reached chapter XXIX, in which Hurstwood steals almost $11,000 from his employers and flees Chicago with Carrie. Dreiser was more than halfway through the novel, and it was time to begin having his manuscript typed for submission to a publisher. Arthur Henry had become quite friendly with Anna Mallon, who would later become his second wife. Anna owned a large and successful typing agency, and she offered to have Henry's and Dreiser's work typed by her stenographers for very reasonable fees.

Dreiser took the first twenty-nine chapters of *Sister Carrie* to Anna's workers; they began typing and he pressed ahead with the rest of the story. The typists were to catch up with him near the end of the book and copy the last few chapters immediately after he composed them. In this way he would be able to show a finished typescript to a prospective publisher shortly after he completed the manuscript.

On the stage, Mrs. Van Dam was making her fond insinuation against Laura.

Carrie listened, and caught the infection of something - she did not know what. Her nostrils sniffed thinly.

> Details from MS.XIX.34 and TS.218: Dreiser had written "proud insinuations," but the typist typed "fond insinuation."

Dreiser's handwritten drafts were difficult to decipher. His cramped, backhanded script was hard to read, and the typists sometimes miscopied his words. There were also frequent instances of "eyeskip"—an error caused when a typist took her eyes from the manuscript page and then resumed typing further down the page. Dreiser caught some of these mistakes, but he was disinclined to check each odd reading back against the manuscript. Instead he substituted another reading and pressed on. These impromptu revisions were often inferior to what he had originally written.

Once these things were in her hand, on her person, she might
dream of giving them up, the method by which they came might intrude
itself so forcefully that she would ache to be rid of the ~~thought~~ of
it, but she would not give them up. "Put on the old clothes - that
torn pair of shoes," was called to her by her conscience in vain.

Details from MS.XI.5 and TS.121: Dreiser wrote "she would ache to be rid of the canker of it," but the typist could not decipher *canker* and left a blank space where Dreiser might fill in the word. Dreiser did not check back in the manuscript for the missing reading; instead he simply substituted the word *thought* in the blank.

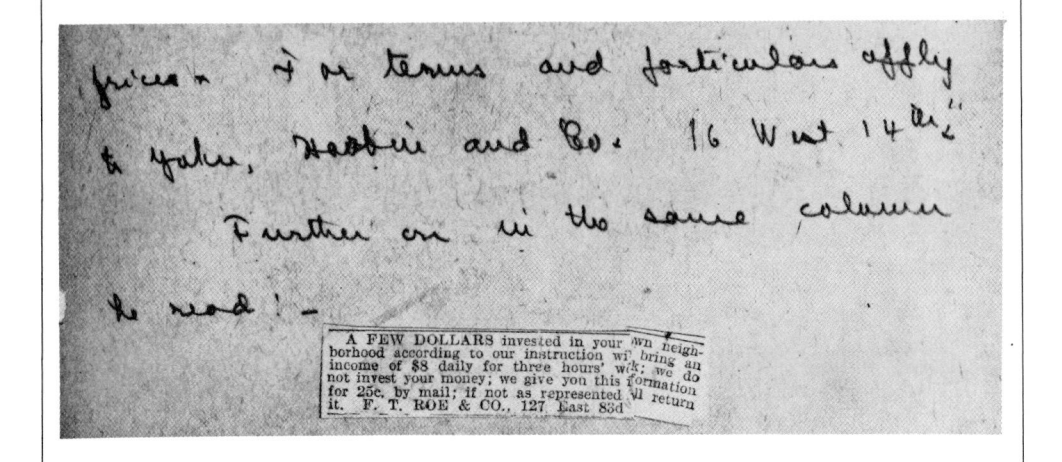

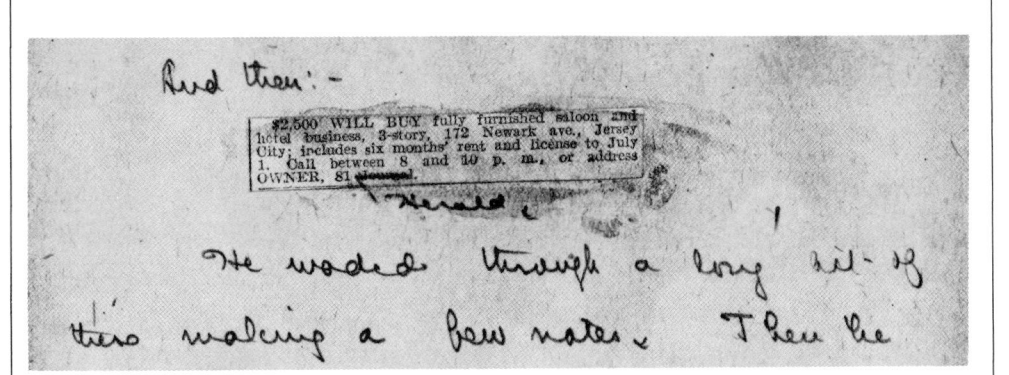

Details from MS.XXXVIII.1 and 2, with classified ads pasted into the text.

As Dreiser neared the end of his manuscript he turned to the newspapers for authentic detail. At this point in the narrative, Hurstwood is searching for investment opportunities in the classified ads. Dreiser clipped actual classified notices from the *New York Journal* and pasted them into his manuscript.

Thinks the Men Will Come to Their Senses by Wednesday.

Things were quiet throughout the day at the general offices of the Atlantic Avenue system, Atlantic and Third Avenues. President Benjamin Norton was early at the office and he at once sent out the following notice, which was posted in every station:

The motormen and conductors and other employes of this company having abruptly left its service, an opportunity is now given to all loyal men who have struck against their will to be reinstated, provided they will make their applications by 12 o'clock noon on Wednesday, Jan. 16. Such men will be given employment (with guaranteed protection) in the order in which such applications are received, and runs and positions assigned them accordingly. Otherwise they will be considered discharged, and every vacancy will be filled by a new man as soon as his services can be secured.

From the *New York Times* account of a streetcar strike in Brooklyn (15 Jan. 1895, p. 2).

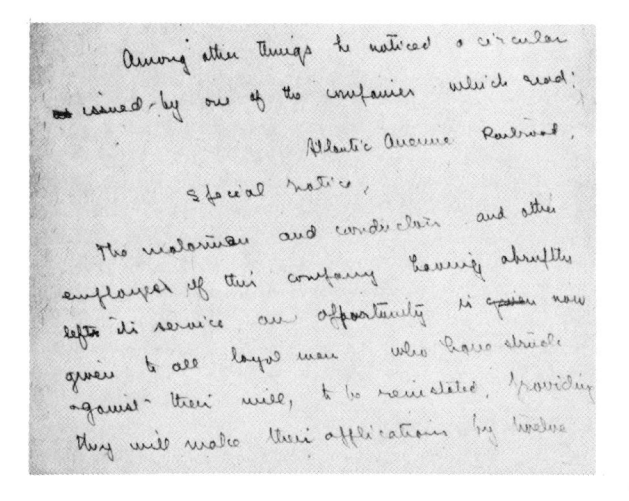

Details from MS. XLIII. 15 and 16: Dreiser incorporates the *Times* notice into his text.

And for the section of *Sister Carrie* in which he describes the streetcar strike, Dreiser copied a notice from the *New York Times* into his manuscript.

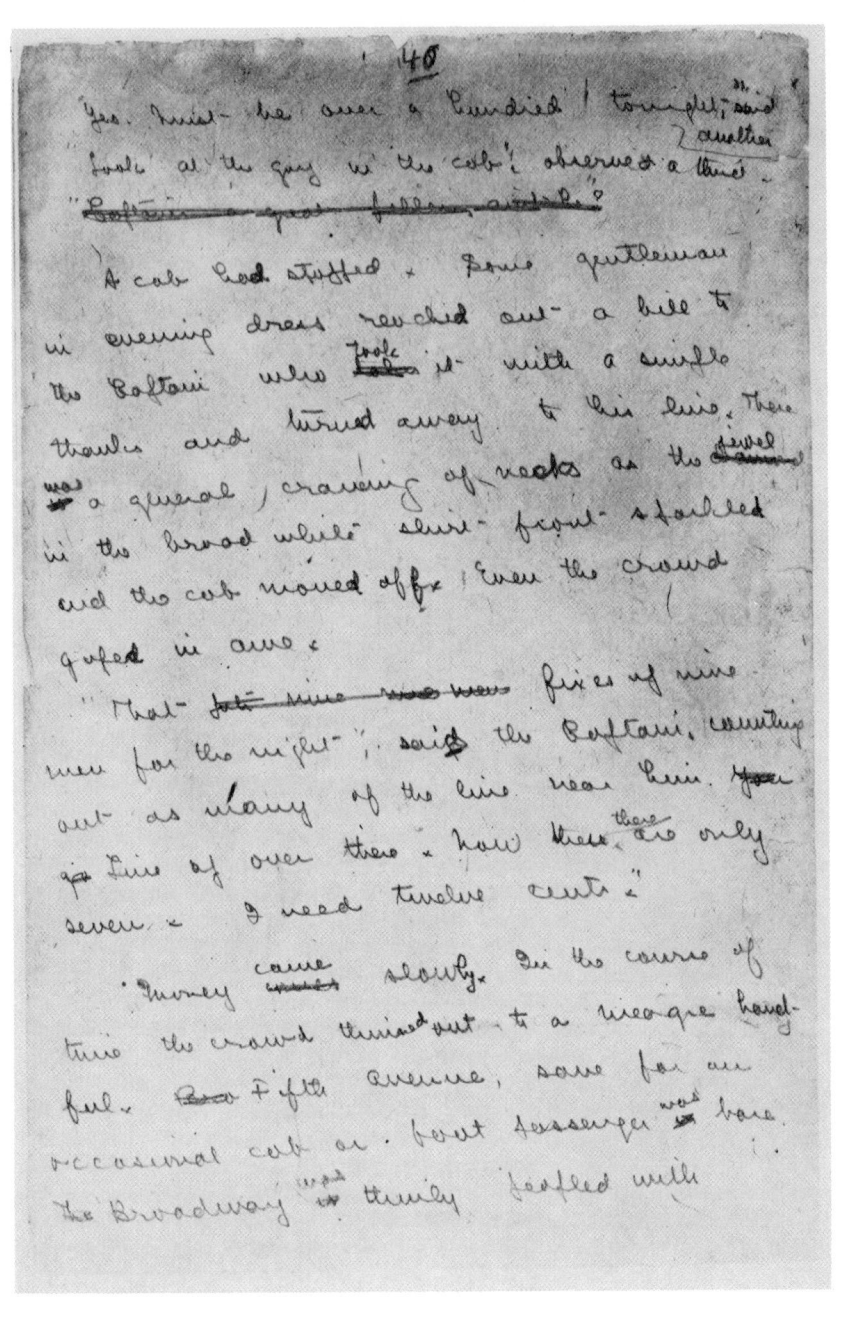

MS.XLVIII.40: This leaf did double duty, first as a leaf of the manuscript of "Curious Shifts" and later as a leaf of the manuscript of *Sister Carrie*. Dreiser changed the verb tenses in order to blend the text into his novel.

In the last two chapters of *Sister Carrie*, Dreiser recycled some of his own writing. He took several leaves from the original manuscript of his article "Curious Shifts of the Poor," already published in *Demorest's*, and spliced them into the manuscript of his novel.

Anna T. Mallon & Co.
Stenographers & Typewriters.

Mutual Reserve Building,
309 Broadway,
New York.

ANNA T. MALLON.   NOTARY PUBLIC.
TEL.CALL 1175 FRANKLIN.

March 22, 1900.

Dear Mr. Author:

      We have finished the last iniquitous chapter of
Sister Carrie, and are now ready for something hot and sizzling.
So please send her down.

          Impatiently,

            THE INFANT CLASS.

This note should have warned Dreiser that his novel might be thought "immoral."

By the time Dreiser finished chapter XLIX, the typists had caught up with him, and on 22 March they sent him a playful note.

MS.L.40: Dreiser's first ending for *Sister Carrie*.

One week later Dreiser finished the manuscript, at 2:53 P.M., with a description of Hurstwood's suicide. Dreiser was satisfied with this ending when he wrote it; he had the last chapter copied by the typists and added it to the other chapters. He was now ready to revise the typescript and submit it to a publisher.

> of the machine. The latter jumped to the task of punching, with sharp snapping clicks, ~~circular~~ *cutting* bits of leather out of the side of the upper, leaving the holes which ~~eventually~~ were to hold the laces. After observing a few times, the girl let her work at it alone. ~~Eventually,~~ *Seeing* that it was fairly *well* done, she went away.
>
> The pieces of leather ~~that she operated upon~~ came from the girl at the machine *To* her ~~left~~ *right*, and were passed on, ~~after being operated upon once more~~ to the girl at her ~~right~~ *left*.. Carrie saw at once

Detail from TS.43: Here Dreiser is simplifying his explanation of Carrie's work in the shoe factory.

> Carrie looked about her, very much disturbed and quite sure that she did not want to work here. ~~No one, outside of~~ *aside from* making her uncomfortable by sidelong glances, *no one* paid her the least attention. She waited ~~quite a few minutes~~ until the whole department was aware of her presence. Then some word was sent around and a foreman, in an apron and shirt sleeves, the latter rolled up to his shoulders, approached.

Detail from TS.29: Dreiser is revising in order to bring together his subject and verb.

Revision of the Typescript

Dreiser worked on the typescript carefully. He knew that he was no stylist—in the conventional sense, at least—and he worked hard to smooth out awkward spots and infelicitous phrasing.

```
        The lack of feeling in the thing was ridiculous.   Carrie

did not get it at all.   She seemed to be talking in her sleep.   It
                          were              a
looked as if she was certain to be wretched failure.   She was more

hapless than Mrs. Morgan, who had recovered somewhat, and was now

saying her lines clearly at least.   Drouet looked away from the
                      audience
stage at the people.   The latter held out silently, hoping for a
```

Detail from TS.215: Jug introduces the subjunctive mode.

```
was his.
                                                    220

        "Fine," he said, and then seized by a sudden impulse, jump-
                                                         arose
ed up and went about to the stage door.

        When he came in upon Carrie, she was still with Drouet.
```

Detail from TS.220: Here Jug "upgrades" Dreiser's verb but in the process alters Hurstwood's action.

```
        "You said Charlie was hurt," said Carrie savagely.    "You
    deceived                    deceiving me
lied to me.    You've been lying all the time and now you want  to

force me to run away with you."
```

Detail from TS.326: Proper young ladies in Jug's day did not use the verb *to lie* as Carrie does here. Jug revised to *deceive*, but in doing so lessened the intensity of Carrie's anger.

Jug went over the typescript for grammar, punctuation, and spelling. She had been a schoolteacher in Ohio, and she knew the formal rules of English grammar. Her insistence that Dreiser's characters observe grammatical niceties in dialogue, however, was probably unfortunate. Her "corrections" in the typescript often gave a false primness to the spoken words.

you

"Won't come have a drink?"

"Not until afterwards," said the exmanager. "I'll see you later. Are you stopping here?"

spoke of;

lending

"Would you mind ~~loaning~~ me the twenty-five dollars you spoke of?"

"Why, no," said Lola, going for her purse.

"How would you like to come in on that with me?" he heard Morrison say.

"Not me," he answered, just as he had years before. "I
have
~~got~~ my hands full now."

Details from TS.339, 522, and 549: Jug's revisions in these three passages remove slang from Dreiser's dialogue.

Carrie had thought ~~some~~ of going for a walk, and had put
with a jaunty double-breasted jacket.
on a light gray woolen dress, ~~the jacket of which was set with a double row of large gray buttons~~. She had ~~gotten~~ out her hat and gloves, ~~which were before her upon the dresser~~, and was fastening a white lace tie about her throat when the housemaid brought up the information that Mr. Hurstwood wished to see her.

Detail from TS.151: A more "creative" revision by Jug, but the phrasing is not typical of Dreiser.

> He seemed rather annoyed at having to bother with such help,
> but put down her name and then led her across to where a line of girls
> ~~was sitting on a line of~~ stools in front of ~~a line of~~ clack-
> ing machines. On the shoulders of one of the girls who was punching

Detail from TS.42: Henry seems not to have recognized Dreiser's deliberate repetition of "a line of" in this sentence. The downturned letter *d* in *occupied* is characteristic of Henry's handwriting.

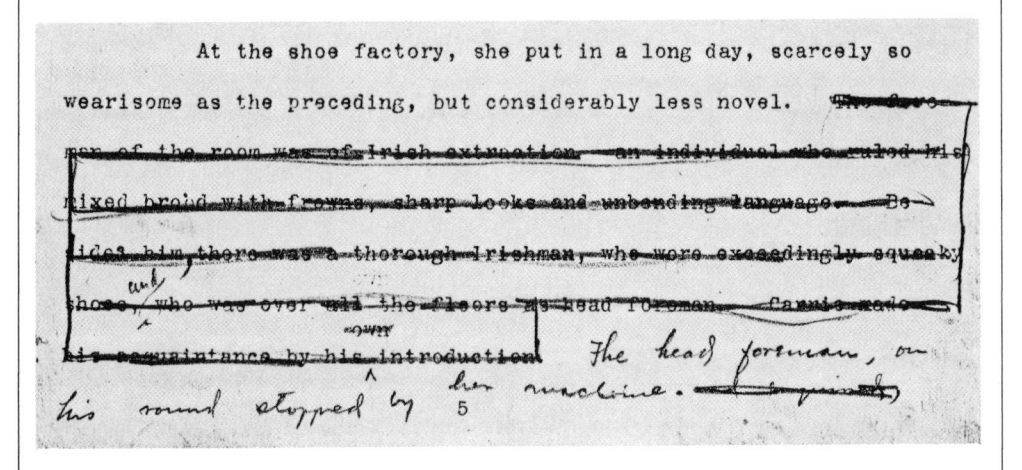

Detail from TS.63: Henry removes details about the two foremen in the shoe factory where Carrie works.

Henry also helped with the revising. He worked over the first two hundred pages carefully, and some of his changes were helpful. He apparently tired of the job, however, for his work is not so careful or so much in evidence in the later chapters of the typescript.

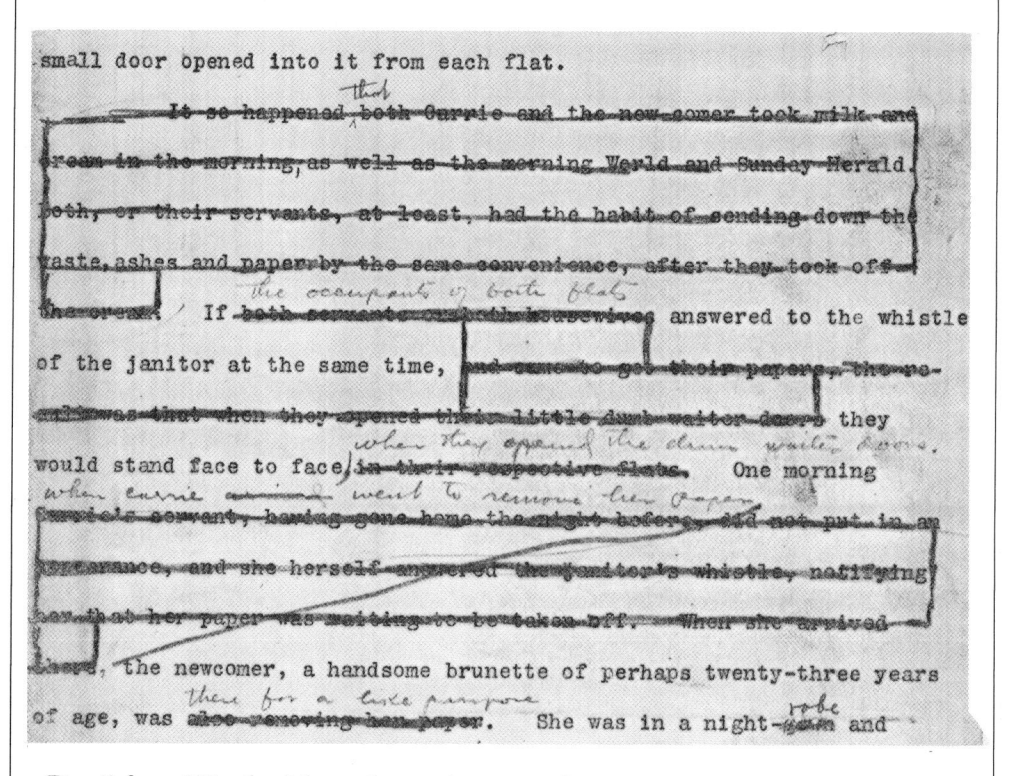

> Carrie looked at her out of the corner of her eye, ~~after she~~
> ~~had answered in the negative.~~ "No" she answered.
>
> "I don't think you'd better try any more this fall," said
> Minnie. ~~[illegible] feeling that Hanson would want Carrie to go back~~

Detail from TS.87: Henry's revision here clarifies a confusing sentence.

> small door opened into it from each flat.
> ~~It so happened~~ _that_ ~~both Carrie and the new-comer took milk and~~
> ~~cream in the morning, as well as the morning World and Sunday Herald.~~
> ~~Both, or their servants, at least, had the habit of sending down the~~
> ~~waste, ashes and paper by the same convenience, after they took off~~
> ~~the cream.~~ _the occupants of both flats_ If ~~both servants or the housewives~~ answered to the whistle
> of the janitor at the same time, ~~and came to get their papers, the re-~~
> ~~sult was that when they opened their little dumb-waiter doors~~ they _when they opened the dumb waiter doors._
> would stand face to face ~~in their respective flats.~~ One morning
> _when Carrie_ ~~[illegible]~~ went to remove her paper
> ~~[illegible] servant, having gone home the night before, did not put in an~~
> ~~appearance, and she herself answered the janitor's whistle, notifying~~
> ~~her that her paper was waiting to be taken off. When she arrived~~
> ~~there,~~ the newcomer, a handsome brunette of perhaps twenty-three years
> of age, was ~~also removing her paper.~~ _there for a like purpose_ She was in a night-~~gown~~ _robe_ and

Detail from TS.369: Heavy internal revising by Henry. The change from
"night-gown" to "night-robe" in the bottom line is by Jug, who apparently felt
that a "night-gown" might be too revealing.

When the world that they represented
no longer allured her (being in itself its
ambassadors (H + D) were discredited.
~~So the best~~ So that now, even
H in his orig. state, would have
not allured her. He was fitted
because of his former self. Would
have disposed of him as she
would have Drouet

— Carrie is an illustration of the
by what devious ways one who
feels, rather than reasons, may be led
in the pursuit - of beauty

— She was waiting for the impossible
- that day when she should led
forth among things which are
dreams merely. Hence her grief.

The first leaf of the notes, in Dreiser's handwriting.

Revision of the Ending

The most intriguing question about *Sister Carrie* concerns the revision
of its ending. At some point after the final chapter was typed, Dreiser
became dissatisfied with his original ending and changed it. His reasons for doing so are unclear and, unless new evidence turns up, are

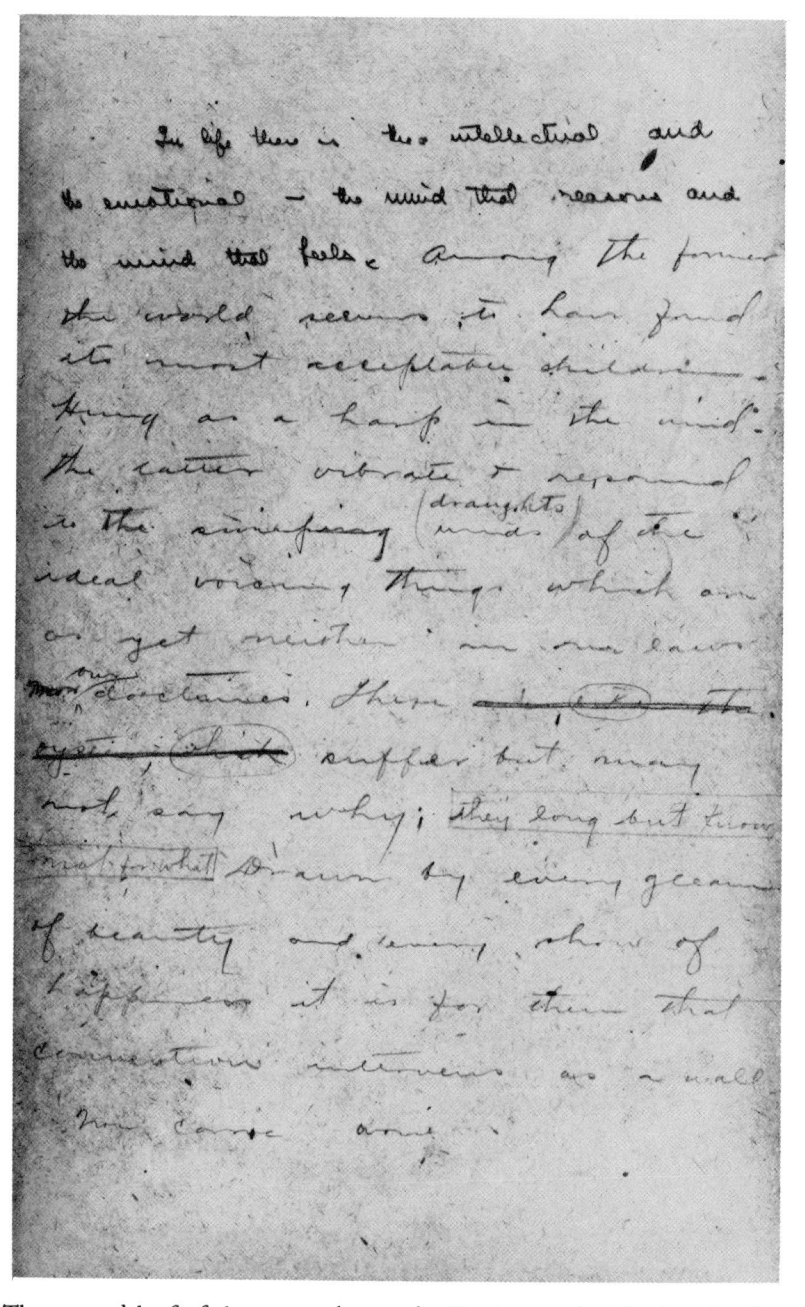

The second leaf of the notes, begun by Dreiser and picked up by Jug.

likely to remain mysterious. The surviving evidence, however, does suggest that Jug and Henry persuaded or influenced him to revise. At the end of the *Sister Carrie* manuscript one finds thirteen leaves of notes about the last two chapters. The entire first leaf is in Dreiser's hand, as is the first sentence on the second leaf, but the remaining leaves are in Jug's handwriting.

The text of the thirteen leaves follows, in diplomatic transcription.

[Leaf 1, in Dreiser's hand]

When the world that they represented no longer allured her (being in it) its ambassadors (H & D) were discredited. The fact   So that now, even H in his orig. state, would have not allured her. He was pitied because of his former self. Would have disposed of him as she would have Drouet

—

Carrie is an illustration of the by what devious ways one who feels, rather than reasons, may be led in the pursuit of beauty

—

She was waiting for the impossible—that day when she should led forth among things which are dreams merely. Hence her grief.

[Leaf 2, begun by Dreiser, finished by Jug]

In life there is the intellectual and the emotional—the mind that reasons and the mind that feels. Among the former the world seems to have found its most acceptable children. Hung as a harp in the wind—the latter vibrate & resound to the sweeping draughts of the ideal voicing things which are
                    winds
as yet neither in our laws nor our doctrines. These suffer but may not say why; they long but know not for what. Drawn by every gleam of beauty and every show of happiness it is for them that convention intervenes as a wall.

Now Carrie wou

[Leaves 3-11, in Jug's hand]

Carrie would walk down B'dway in what mood.? In midst of shine & glitter that had attracted now that she is as in them and part of them, what effect? The [unreadable word] spoke

36

as loudly as before but she heard not—she was hearkening to other voices—

She was even more pathetic than before—She was unsophisticated [unreadable word] coming to Chicago—All these things were beckoning to her—moving her to tears—yet the things she then longed for were taught   The wall then was so strong she was moved to tears—but then the strings that called were—material. The mansions, the carriage, fine clothes, the appearance of the world when thing which some already had secured—From her far away view she could see the glamor and the glint—Drawn near and set down among them—in nature the glint is seen on the trees—you approach and it is gone—only to be found on the next and more distant tree—This is no less true of men than material objects.

The time was when Drouet, Hurstwood represented for her those thing which are worth while but not only in these things in men—They were the agents—They were the personal representations of these things—They were the titled ambassadors of comfort peace aglow with their credentials XXXXXXX

Ames is not a matrimonial possibility—That is not his significance   Had she never seen him after his first the effect would have been great—in as much as he opened up for her a further vista—Her last meeting had given voice—expression that she now felt her—She realized that what she had was not what she wanted—

The feeling that the part she was playing was nothing—was simply emphasized by realizing his attitude toward it. She had, herself a dormant desire of her own to a

She was in her own motive and disposition just such a character as you'd find moving in a strong conventional comedy drama   His direct that she should do this had served to fixed her longing definitely on that thing—always on something better. as But even as she would contemplate this her desire would change again into vague longings—after.

She was because of all this a distinct figure. Sum up the various things that make life busy for Lilian Russell type that didn't appeal to her. For this [unreadable word] she preferred to be alone—It is impossible to conceive of a situation in which such a nature would be altogether joyous and content—only momentairly—

If she were put where daily her mind would be fed with new possibilities—new ideas—it is conceivable that she would be at least contented—a contentment at best tinged with melancholy—
When she parted with Ames that her nature was stirred again to unrest. He had served only to awaken new possibilities. To suggest the better way that seemed almost impossible to follow—
She had become the old mournful Carrie—with the unsatisfied longing—Finish of Chapter XLIX.
Beginning Chapter 51
Carrie never knew of Hurstwood's death—It passed her notice. There were times when moved by an emotion of pity she thot of him & would have sought him out had she know where to seek, & helped him—

Carrie in her new state was much the same Carrie—She was no longer walking the street & looking with wonder & longing—on the outside—

every doorway a bar—a sealed entrance to a garden of delight. She now sat inside the chambers—

It was now the garden within. Looking outward—Instead of flying around Helter skelter with the rest of those who made up her world [the words *her world* in Dreiser's hand]

what delight she know was found in he quiet rocker in her room—

Castle upon Castle—receding in the Western light—aglow & aglint with all the colors of fancy—Dream boats and swan songs—such joys as never were—

While Lola was doing this that or other there she sat, if happy—humming a little tune—
If thot's of the life she had left came to her—

These are random notes, written hastily, but they do focus on two particular points: the notion that Ames has mistakenly been presented as a "matrimonial possibility" for Carrie in chapter XLIX, and the feeling that *Sister Carrie* should not end with Hurstwood's suicide. Some of the phrasing in these notes reappears in the revised ending of the novel.

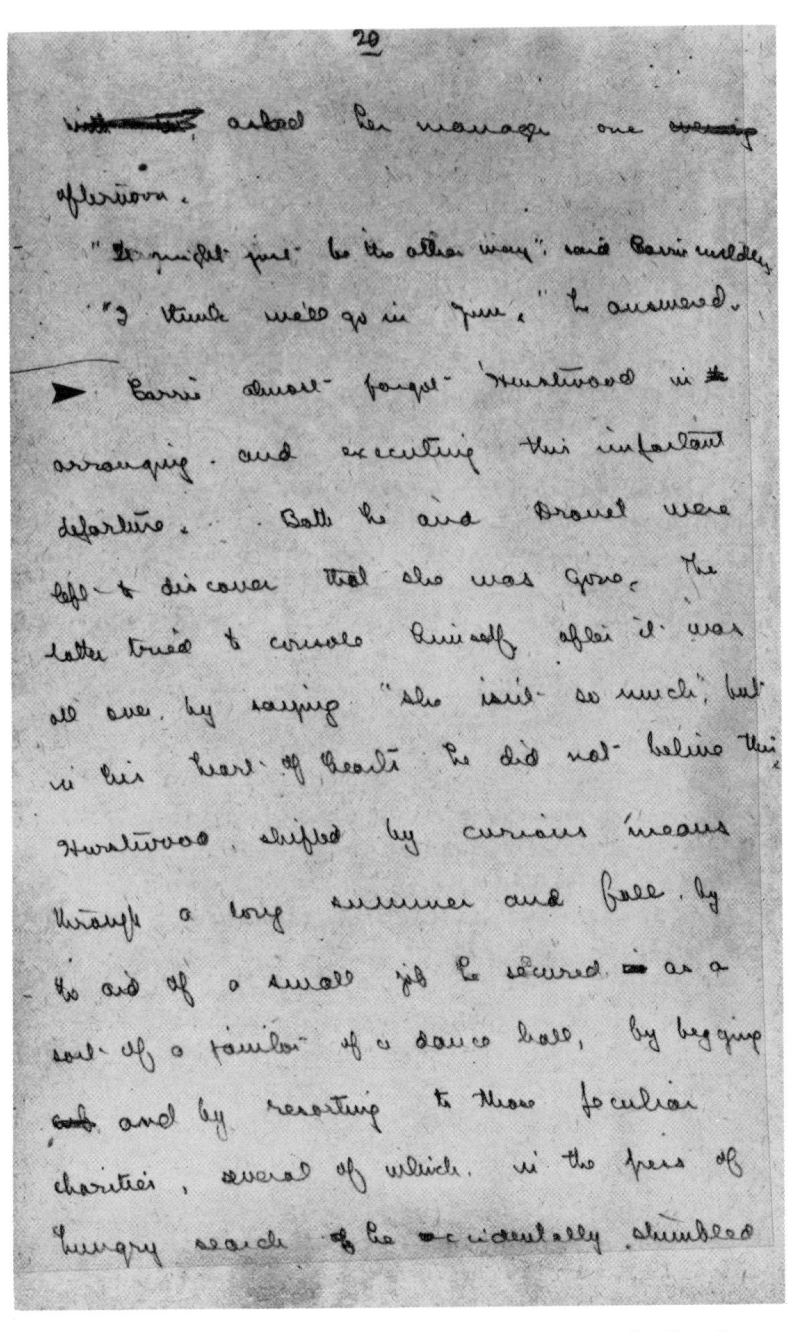

MS.XLIX.20, from the original draft of chapter XLIX. The line in the left margin indicates that Dreiser will rewrite from this point on.

First Dreiser rewrote the ending of chapter XLIX. He discarded the old manuscript leaves and wrote a new version of the meeting between Carrie and Ames at Mrs. Vance's party. In the new scene, Ames is not nearly so attracted to Carrie, and there is no suggestion that they will see each other again.

MS.XLIX.1(rev): The first leaf of the rewritten ending for chapter XLIX.

MS.XLIX.49: The first version of the "blind strivings" passage, from the original ending of chapter XLIX.

Dreiser also added a coda to the end of his book, a meandering philosophical conclusion in which he directed the reader's attention to Carrie. He seems to have been at a loss for heightened language with which to end this coda, however, so he salvaged the discarded final paragraph of the original ending of chapter XLIX and transferred it, rewritten, to the end of the book.

MS. L. unpaginated: Dreiser's revision of the "blind strivings" passage, from the new ending of chapter L.

The first page of Jug's recopied (and revised) version of the coda.

Dreiser had finished revising the ending, but his own draft of the coda was filled with revisions and interlinings. He therefore asked Jug to inscribe a fair copy for the typist. She did so, but in the process of recopying she made changes in the text. She may or may not have

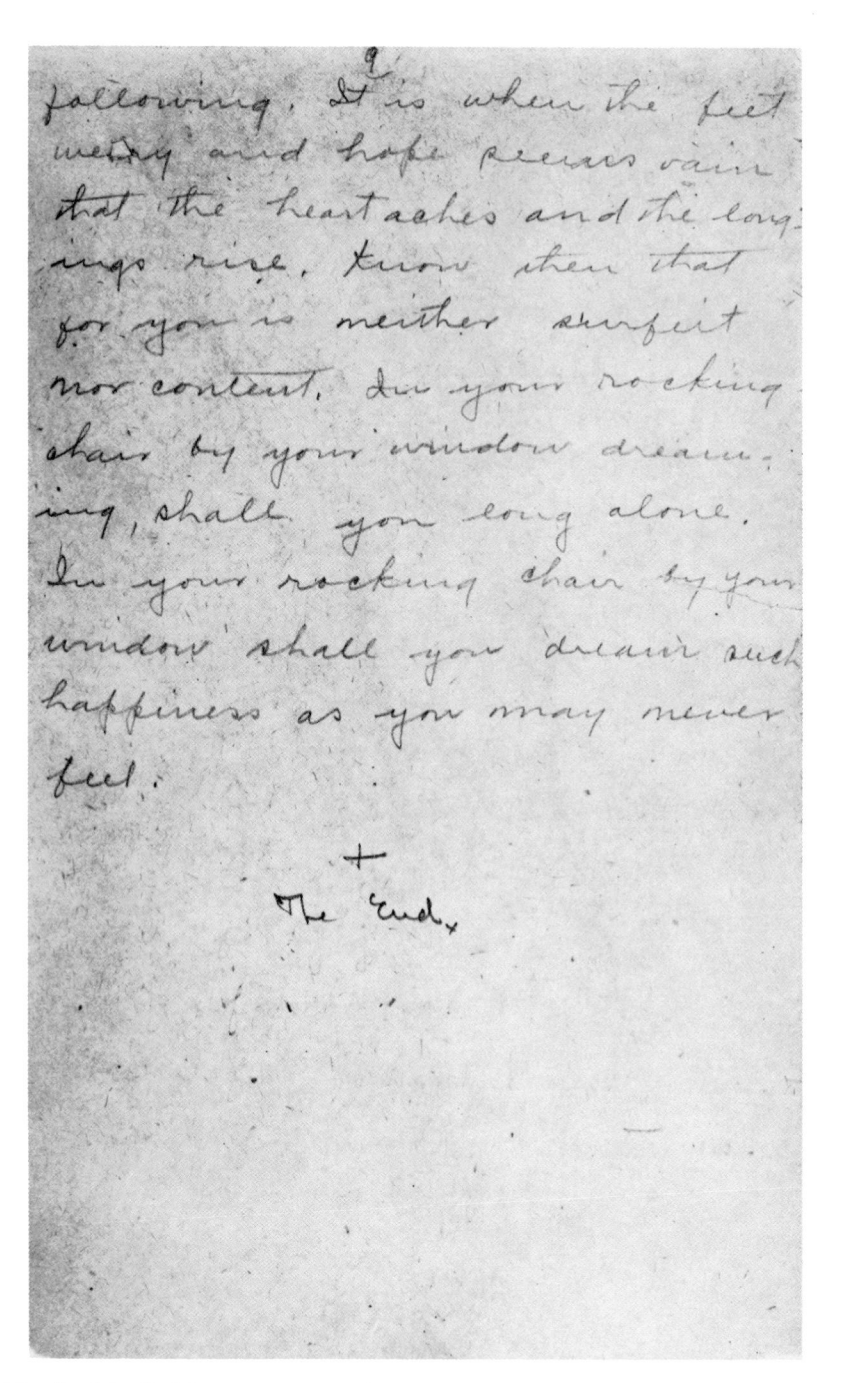

The final leaf of Jug's revision of the coda. Dreiser has added "The End."

revised with Dreiser's consent—the manuscript provides no clues—but her changes were significant. Jug's ending was typed by one of Anna Mallon's stenographers and eventually appeared in the published book. In fact, Jug's ending was the only ending ever printed in a text of *Sister Carrie* before 1981.

Sitting alone, she was now an illustration of the devious
ways by which one who feels rather than reasons, may be led in the
pursuit of beauty.   Though often disillusioned, she was still waiting
for that halcyon day when she should be led forth among dreams become real.   Ames had pointed out a farther step, but on and on beyond
that, if accomplished, would lie others for her.   It was forever to
be the pursuit of that radiance of delight which tints the distant
hilltops of the world.

        O Carrie, Carrie!   Oh blind strivings of the human heart.
Onward, onward it saith, and where beauty leads, there it follows.
Whether it be the tinkle of a lone sheep bell o'er some quiet landscape or the glimmer of beauty in sylvan places, or the show of soul
in some passing eye, the heart knows and makes answer, following.
It is when the feet weary and hope seems vain that the heartaches
and the longings rise.   Know then that for you is neither surfeit
nor content.   In your rocking chair by your window dreaming, shall
you long alone.   In your rocking chair by your window shall you
dream such happiness as you may never feel.

                        The End.

                        15

Details from TS.597 and
from p. 557 of the first edition:
Jug's ending in typescript
and in print.

Sitting alone, she was now an illustration of the devious ways by which one who feels, rather than reasons, may be led in the pursuit of beauty. Though often disillusioned, she was still waiting for that halcyon day when she should be led forth among dreams become real. Ames had pointed out a farther step, but on and on beyond that, if accomplished, would lie others for her. It was forever to be the pursuit of that radiance of delight which tints the distant hilltops of the world.

Oh, Carrie, Carrie! Oh, blind strivings of the human heart! Onward, onward, it saith, and where beauty leads, there it follows. Whether it be the tinkle of a lone sheep bell o'er some quiet landscape, or the glimmer of beauty in sylvan places, or the show of soul in some passing eye, the heart knows and makes answer, following. It is when the feet weary and hope seems vain that the heartaches and the longings arise. Know, then, that for you is neither surfeit nor content. In your rocking-chair, by your window dreaming, shall you long, alone. In your rocking-chair, by your window, shall you dream such happiness as you may never feel.

THE END

Henry Mills Alden, who read
Sister Carrie in typescript and liked it, but
predicted that it would be too frank
for Harper & Bros. to publish.

The Harper reader's report.
The penciled annotations are by Dreiser.

Criticism from Harper
Rendered May 2nd 1900
Took novel to Doubleday & Page

This is a superior piece of reporterial realism - of highclass newspaper work,
such as might have been done by George Ade. It contains many elements of strength -
it is graphic, the local color is excellent, the portrayal of a certain below-the-
surface life in the Chicago of twenty years ago faithful to fact. There are chapters that reveal a very keen insight into this phase of life and incidents that dis-
close a sympathetic appreciation of the motives of the characters of the story.
But when this has been said there remains the feeling that the author has not risen
to the standard necessary for the efficient handling of the theme. His touch is
neither firm enough nor sufficiently delicate to depict without offense to the
reader the continued illicit relations of the heroine. The long succession of
chapters dealing with this important feature of the story begin to weary very quickly.
Their very realism weakens and hinders the development of the plot. The final
scenes in New York are stronger and better - But I cannot conceive of the book
arousing the interest or inviting the attention, after the opening chapters, of the
feminine readers who control the destinies of so many novels.

The style is uneven. At times singularly good (and generally so,) it is
disfigured by such colloquialisms as "suspicioned," "pulled off on schedule time,"
"stowed off," "it's up to you," etc.

The Search for a Publisher

Through his friend Henry Mills Alden, editor of *Harper's Monthly*,
Dreiser submitted his finished typescript to Harper & Bros. in early
April 1900. The novel was rejected three weeks later.

47

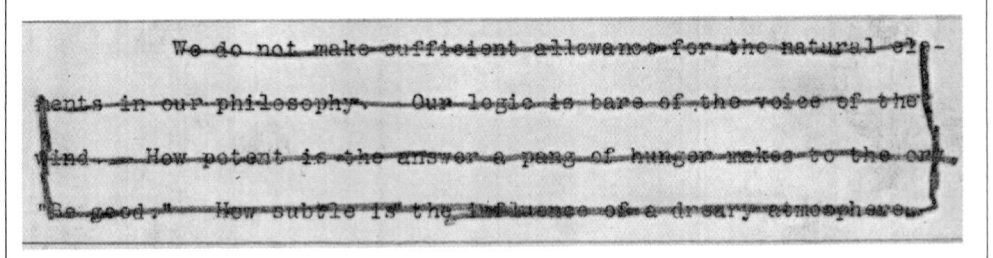

Detail from TS.112: This cut removes a brief but significant philosophical passage.

Dreiser apparently considered the Harper reader's report a caveat to cut and expurgate his typescript. The plot of *Sister Carrie*, he now thought, must be quickened; the sexual passages must be toned down. Henry therefore went through the typescript and marked over 30,000 words for removal. Dreiser approved nearly all of the excisions, balking at only a few. When the cutting process was complete, *Sister Carrie* was a very different work of art.

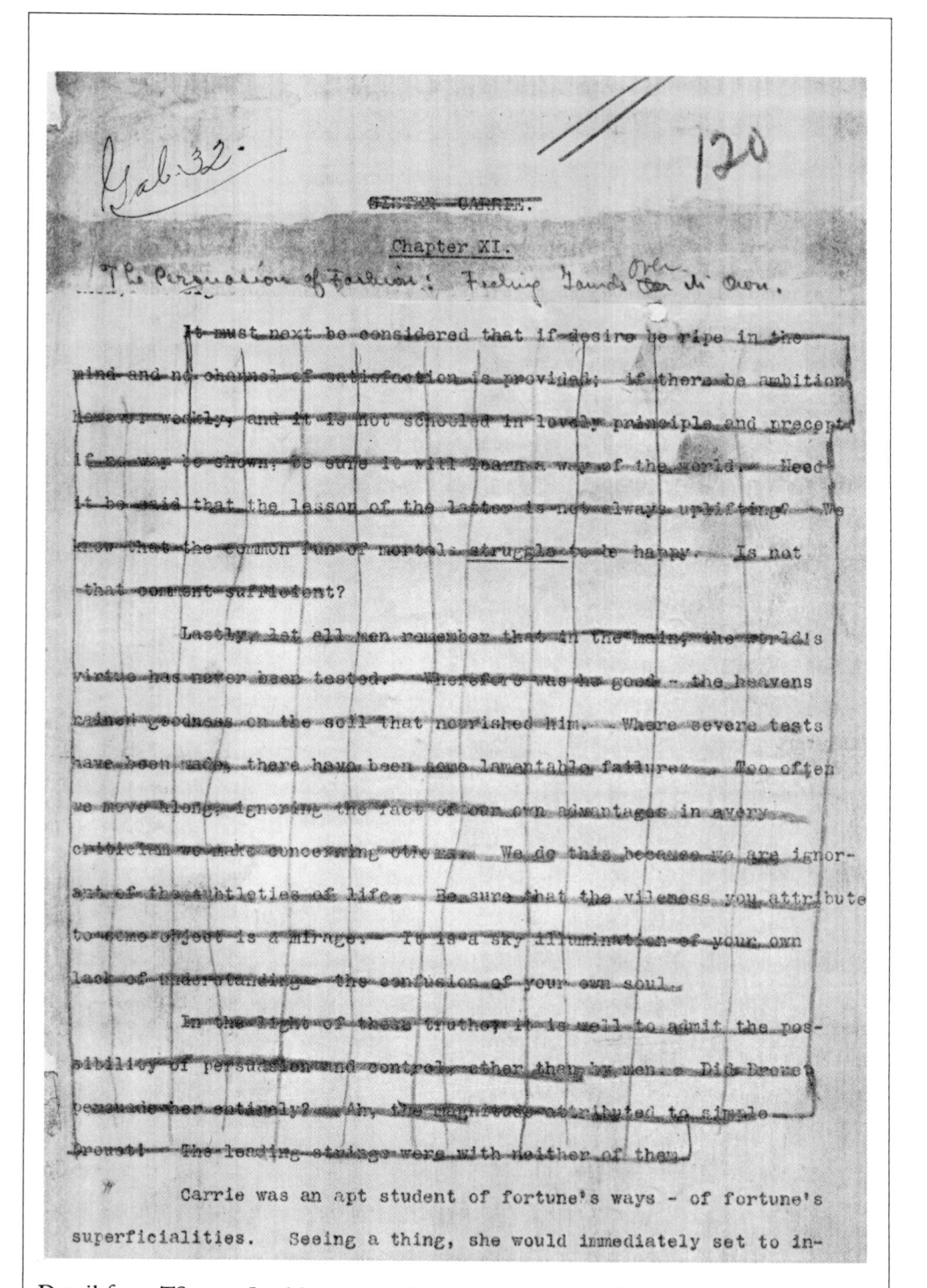

Detail from TS. 120: In this passage Dreiser had explained Carrie's seduction in philosophically naturalistic terms. Henry's brackets (indicating that the section should be cut) were erased, but they are still faintly visible in the left margin of the original.

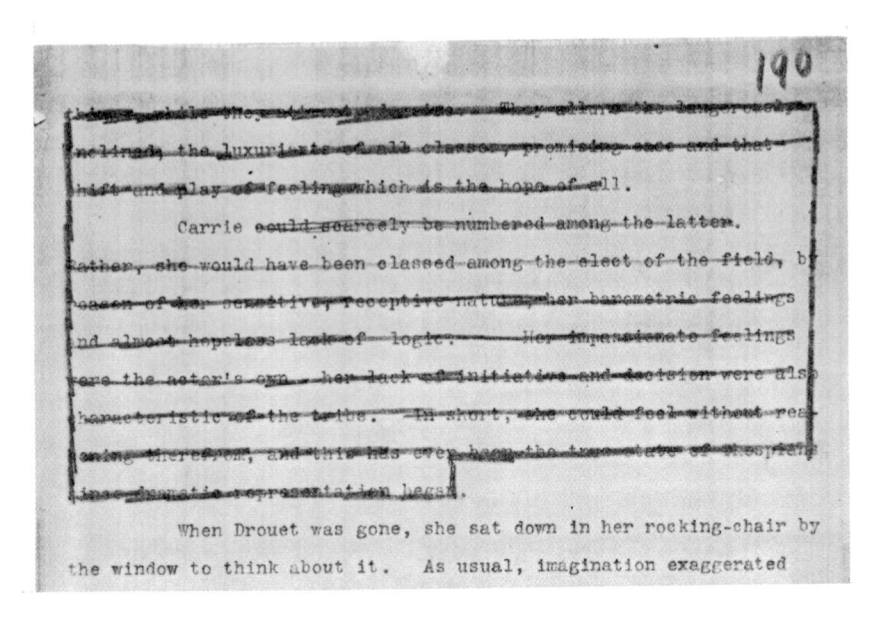

~~inclined the luxuries of all classes, promising ease and that shift and play of feeling which is the hope of all.~~

~~Carrie could scarcely be numbered among the latter. Rather, she would have been classed among the elect of the field, by reason of her sensitive, receptive nature, her barometric feelings and almost hopeless lack of logic. Her impassionate feelings were the actor's own. Her lack of initiative and decision were also characteristic of the tribe. In short, she could feel without reasoning therefrom, and this has ever been the state of the player since dramatic representation began.~~

When Drouet was gone, she sat down in her rocking-chair by the window to think about it. As usual, imagination exaggerated

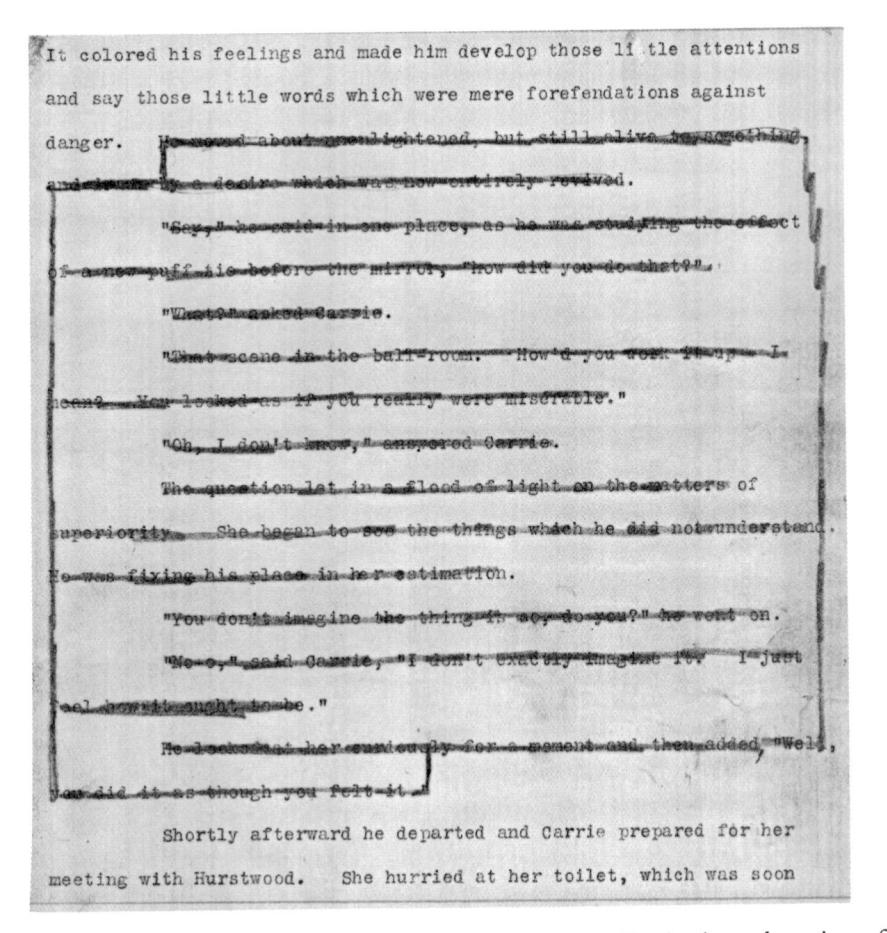

It colored his feelings and made him develop those little attentions and say those little words which were mere forefendations against danger. ~~He moved about, unenlightened, but still alive to something, and drawn by a desire which was now entirely revived.~~

~~"Say," he said in one place, as he was studying the effect of a new puff tie before the mirror, "how did you do that?"~~

~~"What?" asked Carrie.~~

~~"That scene in the ball-room. How'd you work it up. I mean. You looked as if you really were miserable."~~

~~"Oh, I don't know," answered Carrie.~~

~~The question let in a flood of light on the matters of superiority. She began to see the things which he did not understand. He was fixing his place in her estimation.~~

~~"You don't imagine the thing, do you?" he went on.~~

~~"No-o," said Carrie, "I don't exactly imagine it. I just feel how it ought to be."~~

~~He looked at her curiously for a moment and then added, "Well, you did it as though you felt it."~~

Shortly afterward he departed and Carrie prepared for her meeting with Hurstwood. She hurried at her toilet, which was soon

Details from TS.190 and 235: These two cuts remove Dreiser's explanation of Carrie's innate acting ability.

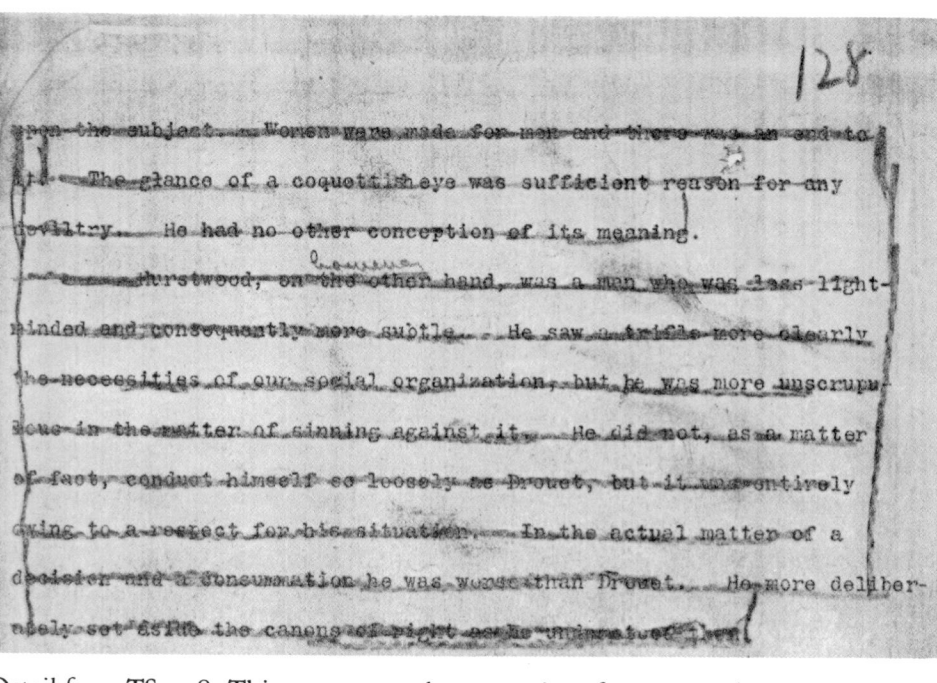

Detail from TS.128: This cut purges the typescript of a passage about Drouet, Hurstwood, and their pursuit of women. Henry's markings in the left margin are easily visible here.

the man beside him.   By the Lord, he could not even applaud feel-

ingly as he would.   For once, he must simulate when it left a taste

in his mouth.

~~In the second act, Carrie had two good situations, one~~
~~with her lover, Ray, who came to win her back; one with her sup-~~
~~posed mother, Judas, who, with her criminal pal, forced her to come~~
~~along against her will.   In the third act, she was tried in a police~~
~~court for disobedience to her "fake" father, forced into a carriage,~~
~~and finally rescued by some water rats and her lover, when being~~
~~brought down to the river at the dead of night.   In the fourth act,~~
~~she was seen under the old circumstances, among friends, but still~~
~~hounded by designing villains and still refusing to take back her~~
~~lover, who wished to restore himself in her regard.~~

It was in ~~this~~ the last act that Carrie's fascination for her lovers

assumed its most effective character.   ~~Drouet had been so carried~~

~~away by the performance that Hurstwood found at the end of the sec-~~

9

Detail from TS.222: This passage furnished detail about Carrie's part in *Under the Gaslight*.

would thrill as a child with the unhindered passion that was in him. He loved the thing that women love in themselves, grace. At this, their own shrine, he knelt with them, an ardent devotee.

"Did you see that woman who went by just now?" he said to Carrie on the ~~very~~ first day they took a walk together.

"Fine stepper, wasn't she?"

Carrie looked ~~again~~ and observed the grace commended.

"Yes, she is," she returned cheerfully, a little suggestion of possible defect in herself awakening in her mind. If that was so fine, she must look at it more closely. Instinctively she felt a desire to imitate it. Surely she could do that too.

When one of her mind sees many thing emphasized and re-emphasized and admired, she gathers the logic of it and applies accordingly. Drouet was not shrewd enough to see that this was not tactful. He could not see that it would be better to make her feel that she was competing with herself, not others better than herself. He would not have done it with an older, wiser woman, but in Carrie he saw only the novice. Less clever than she, he was naturally unable to comprehend her sensibility. He went on educating and ~~wondering~~ ^{wounding} her, a thing rather foolish in one whose admiration for his pupil and victim was apt to grow.

Carrie took the instructions affably. She saw what Drouet liked; in a vague way she saw where he was weak. It lessens a woman's opinion of a man when she learns that his admiration is so pointedly and generously distributed. She sees but one object of supreme compliment in this world, and that is herself. If a man is to succeed with many women, he must be all in all to each.

In her own apartments Carrie saw things which were lessons in the same school.

TS. 122: The passages in this section were reduced so heavily that Dreiser had to use elaborate cut-and-paste methods. The arrows indicate splices.

Frank Norris.

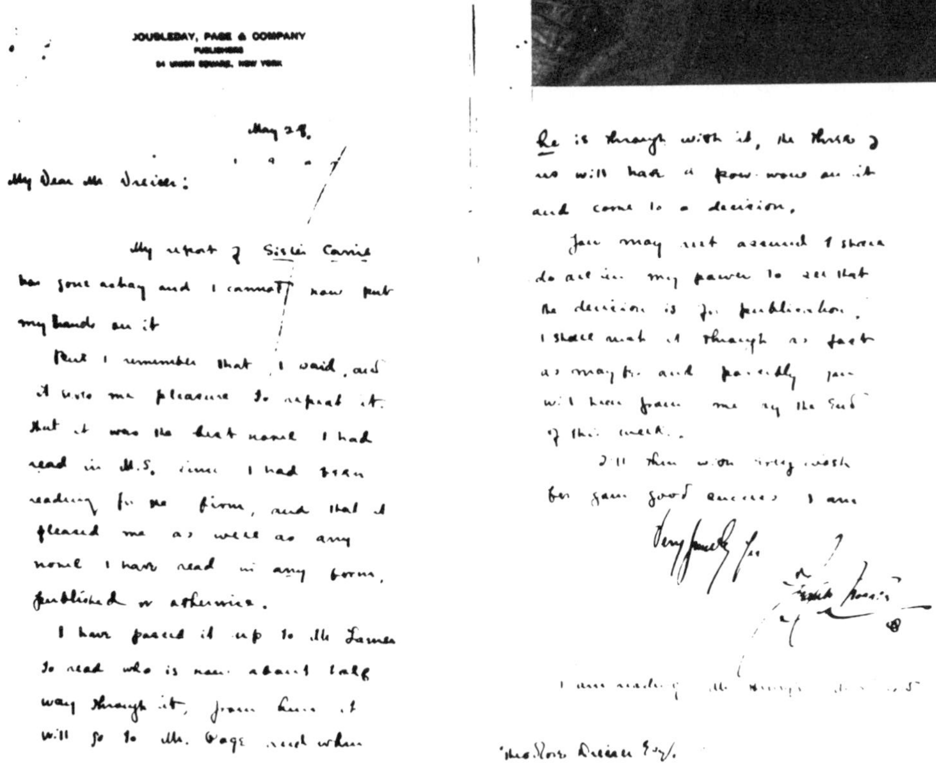

DOUBLEDAY, PAGE & COMPANY
PUBLISHERS
34 UNION SQUARE, NEW YORK

May 28.

My Dear Mr Dreiser:

My report of Sister Carrie has gone astray and I cannot now put my hand on it.

But I remember that I said, and it gives me pleasure to repeat it, that it was the best novel I had read in M.S. since I had been reading for the firm, and that it pleased me as well as any novel I have read in any form, published or otherwise.

I have passed it up to Mr Lanier to read who is now about half way through it, from here it will go to Mr. Page and when he is through with it, the three of us will have a pow-wow over it and come to a decision.

You may rest assured I shall do all in my power to see that the decision is for publication. I shall rush it through as fast as may be and possibly you will hear from me by the end of this week.

I'll then with every wish for your good success I am

Very Sincerely Yrs
Frank Norris

Theodore Dreiser Esq.

Norris's famous letter to Dreiser. His original reader's report, which Norris says has "gone astray," has never been found.

A New Publisher

Dreiser decided to try a younger and more adventurous publishing house, and at Alden's suggestion he took *Sister Carrie* to Doubleday, Page & Co. The novel was read there by Frank Norris, whose own naturalistic novel *McTeague* had just been published by Doubleday. Norris was much taken by *Sister Carrie* and recommended enthusiastically that it be accepted.

Walter Hines Page.

une, 1900.

Dear Sir: As, we hope, Mr. Norris has informed you, we are very much pleased with your novel. If you will be kind enough to call here on Monday — preferably later than two o'clock, we shall be glad to talk it over with

you. With congratulations on so good a piece of work, we are very sincerely yours, Doubleday, Page & Co. by Walter H. Page

Theodore Dreiser Esq

Page's invitation to Dreiser.

Henry Lanier, senior editor at Doubleday, Page & Co., read the typescript and seems to have liked it, though he recommended that the title be changed. He was also wary of printing real names in the novel. Lanier passed the typescript on to Walter Hines Page, junior partner in the firm. The senior partner, Frank Doubleday, was traveling abroad with his wife and was not expected back until July. Page wrote Dreiser an encouraging note and invited him to come by for a talk. The conference went pleasantly, and Dreiser was assured that his novel would be on the Doubleday, Page list for the fall season. No formal contract was signed, however. Dreiser and Jug went on vacation in Montgomery City; they were visiting her parents there when the trouble with Frank Doubleday began.

55

Frank Doubleday.

The Doubleday Affair

Frank Doubleday and his wife returned early in July. Doubleday read *Sister Carrie* in typescript and, for reasons that are obscure, developed a strong dislike for the book. He may have been influenced by his wife, but there is no hard evidence to support that speculation.

56

New York, July 14, 1900.

Dear Teddy:

Yesterday, I had a hot time up at Doubleday & Page's. In talking with Norris, he suggested that I see Lenier, and ask him when he was going to publish your book, as they ought to be getting about it. I asked Lenier, and he said that he didn't know - that he hadonly been back a little while, and hadn't got around to it yet. Norris also suggested that I speak to Lenier about changing the names from those of real people to fictitious ones. Lenier wants all of them changed. He don't want Frohman or Daly, or the real names of newspapers or any of those things. The fact is, that Lenier is a good deal of a cad. He knows nothing at all of real life -his nature is very shallow, and he is exceedingly conceited. We had a very warm argument on the subject. He said that it seemed that all those things seemed to him like a straining after realism. I told him that any one to whom could get such an impression from that book must, in the nature of things, be mistaken, because I knew for a certainty that there had been no straining for realism; and that, on the other hand, were the names of Frohman and Daly, and the news-papers to be changed, that here would be an actual straining, and that, in my opinion, were you to do it, you would stultify yourself.

I presume that the name of Hannah & Hogg will have to be changed because of the crime you have enacted there. For my part, I can see no reason for changing any other thing in the book, and several against it. They also want the name of the book changed. They do not like "Sister Carrie." They think it ought to havea more imposing and pretensious name. This may be true, if you can get a good one.*

I was up to Norris's the other night, on his invitation; Mrs. Norris had just read your story, and we there discussed among ourselves the idea of changingx giving the theatrical managers fic-titious names. Mrs. Norris didn't think that it was at all necessary and Norris himself thinks that it is immaterial, one way or the other In talking over the matter, he said to me that he didn't think you ought to stand in the way of such changes if the matter were made a serious issue. I told Norris that I thought you were the man who had the right to take a stand in the matter. However, this is all f for you to decide, and Norris has asked me to write to you and find out what you will do about it. Lenier intimated to me that he would be opposed to publishing the book unless these vhanges were made.

The first page of Henry's 14 July 1900 letter to Dreiser.

Doubleday attempted to have his firm renege on its commitment to publish *Sister Carrie*. Henry represented the absent Dreiser in the dispute: a flurry of correspondence passed between the two, and also between Dreiser and Page. On Henry's advice, Dreiser stood firm and insisted that Doubleday publish his novel.

Montgomery City.
Mo.

Monday, July   1900.

My Dear Henry: -

Your letter has not disturbed me at all - at least - no more so than if the intelligence concerned another person. I had a forewarning of this, as I shall detail later, about a week ago. Your letter came yesterday noon, and at five P.M. it was followed by Page. As you suggested he is the height of insincerity. He now magnifies some remarks of his concerning the book of which I told you the day we visited Martin and finds the work, — vitally defective. The letter I mail to you herewith, wishing

The first page of Dreiser's answer to Henry.

58

DOUBLEDAY, PAGE & COMPANY
PUBLISHERS
34 UNION SQUARE, NEW YORK

July 19th, 1900.

Dear Mr. Dreiser:

I told you that we would publish " Sister Carrie"; but, since you went away, we have had an opportunity, which had not presented itself before, thoroughly to discuss the book; and the more we have discussed it, I am sorry to report to y u, the more uncertain do we all feel about it. The feeling has grown upon us that, excellent as your workmanship is, the choice of your characters has been unfortunate. I think I told you that, personally, this kind of people did not interest me, and we find it hard to believe they will interest the great majority of readers. We all feel, too, that the mention of real names and places is a mistake, because it destroys the illusion and reduces the story, as it seems to us, more nearly to the level of a mere narrative.

I do not mean, however, to repeat these

The first page of Page's 19 July 1900 letter, in which he attempts to persuade Dreiser to release Doubleday, Page & Co. from its commitment to publish.

Montgomery City
Mo.

July 23rd 1900.

My dear Mr. Page:-

~~Your astonishing letter is before~~

~~me.~~ To say that I am astonished
by the intelligence which your letter of the
19th conveys, is but putting it mildly. I
have, however, given the situation very
serious consideration, and find that
the question of ideas will not need
~~at the~~ an answer from me, until
another phase of the situation has been
looked into. This I herewith present.

Outside of the matter of preserving
your own interest, I am loath to believe

The first leaf of Dreiser's answer to Page. This is the rough draft, which Dreiser kept; presumably he sent a fair copy to Page.

Memorandum of Agreement

Theodore Dreiser Esq, of *New York —*

hereinafter called "the author," being the author and proprietor of a work entitled
"The Flesh & the Spirit" or Sister Carrie

hereby grants and assigns to Doubleday, Page & Co. the above mentioned work, and also all rights of translation, abridgment, dramatization, selection, and other rights of, in, or to said work. Doubleday, Page & Co. shall also have the exclusive right to take out copyright for the said work, and to obtain all renewals of copyright and to hold said copyrights and renewals, and to publish said work during the terms thereof.

No payment shall be made by Doubleday, Page & Co. for permission gratuitously given to publish extracts from said work to benefit the sale thereof ; but if Doubleday, Page & Co. receive any compensation for the publication of extracts therefrom, or for translations, abridgments, or dramatizations, such compensation shall be equally divided between the parties hereto.

The author guarantees that the work is original, and in no way an infringement upon the copyright of others. Also that it contains no libelous statements. And that the author and *his* legal representatives shall and will hold harmless the said Doubleday, Page & Co. from all suits and all manner of claims and proceedings which may be taken on the ground that the said work is such violation or contains anything libelous.

Doubleday, Page & Co., in consideration of the rights granted, agree to publish the work at their own expense, in such a style or styles as they deem most advisable, and to pay the author, or *his* legal representatives, a royalty of ten per cent. on the retail price, cloth style, on all copies sold ~~after~~ ~~copies have been sold, 12½ of~~

It is understood and agreed that no royalty shall be paid on any copies given away, or destroyed, or sold at a price below cost. Also that but half royalty shall be paid on copies sold in foreign countries, at special edition prices.

Expense of author's corrections exceeding ten per cent. of cost of composition shall be charged against the author's account, and it is agreed that the author shall furnish an index, if required, at *his* expense.

Statements of sale shall be rendered semi-annually, in the months of February and August, and settlement thereof shall be made in cash four months later.

It is agreed that Doubleday, Page & Co. shall furnish to the author free of charge ten copies of the work as published ; and should the author desire any more copies for *his* own use, they shall be supplied at one-half the retail price. It is understood and agreed that any copies thus purchased shall not be sold again.

It is further understood and agreed that after a lapse of two years should the work, in the opinion of the said Doubleday, Page & Co., become unsalable, the said Doubleday, Page & Co. may then melt up or destroy the plates. It is understood and agreed that in this case the author may purchase the said plates at cost should *he* desire to do so. In case the author buys the plates under this provision he shall not have the right to use any illustrations furnished by Doubleday, Page & Co. without special agreement between the parties hereto.

This contract may be assigned by either party, but only as a whole, and no part of their respective interests shall be assigned by either party. No assignment of the author shall be valid, as against Doubleday, Page & Co., unless and until they shall have received due evidence thereof in writing.

Executed this *Twentieth*
day of *August* 190*0*

Theodore Dreiser

Witness:

Frank Norris

Doubleday Page Company

The contract for publication of *Sister Carrie*, signed by Dreiser and witnessed by Norris. Dreiser has added the words "or Sister Carrie" to the title line. The terms for escalating royalties have been marked out, perhaps because Doubleday, Page & Co. expected to print only 1,000 copies.

In mid-August Doubleday, on legal advice, gave in and agreed to publish *Sister Carrie*—but not necessarily to advertise or promote the book. On 20 August 1900 a contract was drawn up.

September 4, 1900.

Mr. Theodore Dreiser,

    309 Broadway, City.

Dear Sir:--

    We have been carefully over your manuscript, and wish to make the following suggestions, which we think are absolutely essential; namely, that the original title of the book shall be kept -- "Sister Carrie" -- and all the names of real persons should be changed. We have marked these in the manuscript, and understood that you had already taken them out. You will notice among these Francis Wilson, Charles Frohman, Schlesinger & Meyer, the Waldorf, the Morton House, Mr. Daly's office, etc. It is absolutely imperative that no real names should appear in the book.

    We call your attention to the fact that New York's parade of fashion from 14th Street to 34th Street on Broadway is a misnomer. We have taken out profanity which we regarded as imperative. You will notice that we have marked several passages in the manuscript with a question mark. These we think could be changed to advantage, and we trust you will agree with us and do this.

    We return the manuscript to you herewith, as we do not wish to come to the necessity of making the changes in type.

Very truly yours,

F. N. Doubleday

Doubleday's 4 September 1900 letter, in which he attempts to compromise with Dreiser.

Doubleday agreed to publish *Sister Carrie* but stipulated that real names in the novel be altered and that all profanity be removed. By now at least two persons had read the typescript in search of "questionable" passages. One reader, probably Lanier, had blue-penciled queries in the margins about profanity, sexual references, and real names. The other reader, who was perhaps Doubleday himself, had marked several objectionable passages in red pen. Dreiser considered each queried passage and usually made a revision, but in several cases he balked and refused to make a change.

The first page of Dreiser's rough draft of a reply to Doubleday.

he would converse ~~with~~ longest and ~~perhaps the~~ most seriously.   He
loved to go out and have a good time once in a while - to go to the
races, the theatres, the sporting entertainments at some of the clubs
~~and those more unmentionable resorts of vice -- the gilded chambers of
shame with which Chicago was then so liberally cursed~~   He kept a
horse and neat trap, had his wife and two ~~small sons~~ well established

[children who were]

"Not a thing."

"Well, come round then."

~~"Is she a blonde?" said Drouet laughing.~~

~~"Come around about twelve," said Hurstwood, ignoring the
question."~~

"I struck a little peach coming in on the train Friday,"
remarked Drouet, by way of parting.   "By George, that's so, I must go
and call on her before I go away."

Details from TS.52 and 57: Dreiser cuts sexual references that the Doubleday,
Page & Co. editor had queried in blue pencil.

> "She was good-looking, wasn't she?" said the manager's
> companion who had not caught all the details of the [game he had 77.
> played.
>
> "Yes, in a way," said the other, sore to think the game
> had been lost. "She'd never make an actress, though. Just another
> ~~pair of tights~~ chorus girl - that's all."

Detail from TS.301: In this scene Carrie has just been turned down in an attempt to get on stage in Chicago. The manager of the theatrical company has made advances to her, and she has rebuffed him. The Doubleday, Page & Co. editor queried the phrase "pair of tights" and Dreiser revised to "chorus girl," a less callous comment.

> I wouldn't be over here takin' chances like these."
>
> "It's hell these days, ain't it?" said the man. "A poor man
> ain't nowhere. You could starve, ~~by Jesus~~, right in the streets and,
> there ain't most no one would help you."

Detail from TS.495: The blue-pencil query in the margin is by the Doubleday, Page & Co. editor; the red-ink instructions to the printer to set "dashes" are apparently by Frank Doubleday.

"Who fired that?" he heard an officer exclaim. "By God,
who did that," both left him running towards a certain building. He
paused a moment and then got down.
"George!" exclaimed Hurstwood weakly
"By God," he said vaguely, "this is too much for me."
He walked nervously to the corner and hurried down a side
street.

Detail from TS. 511: Dreiser did not change the first "By God" but revised the second to "George!" three lines below.

Whatever a man like Hurstwood could be in Chicago, it is
very evident that he would be but an inconspicuous drop in an ocean
like New York.   In Chicago, whose population still ranged about
500,000, the Armours, Pullmans, Palmers, Fields had not yet arrived,
as it were.   Millionaires were not numerous.   The rich had not

Detail from TS. 352: Here Dreiser removes the names of well-known Chicago millionaires from his novel.

> "They want a girl, probably, at ten a week," he said.
>
> *gali 108.* Being about one o'clock, he thought of eating and went to a *restaurant in Madison Square* There he pondered over places which he might look up, ~~he could think of some already.~~ He was tired. It was blowing up gray again. Across the way, through Madison Square Park, stood the *great hotels* ~~, looking down upon a busy scene. He decided to go over there in the lobby and sit a while. Accordingly when through, he proceeded there.~~ It was warm in there and bright. He had seen no *he knew* one at the Broadway ~~already.~~ In all likelihood he would encounter

Detail from TS.418: Dreiser alters references to actual restaurants and hotels in New York.

> The advertisements were already in the papers; the posters upon the bill-boards. *The leading lady* ~~Miss Lillian Russell~~ and many members were cited. Carrie was nothing.
>
> As in Chicago, she was seized with stage fright as the very first entrance of the ballet approached, but later she recovered.

Detail from TS.465: "Miss Lillian Russell" becomes "The leading lady."

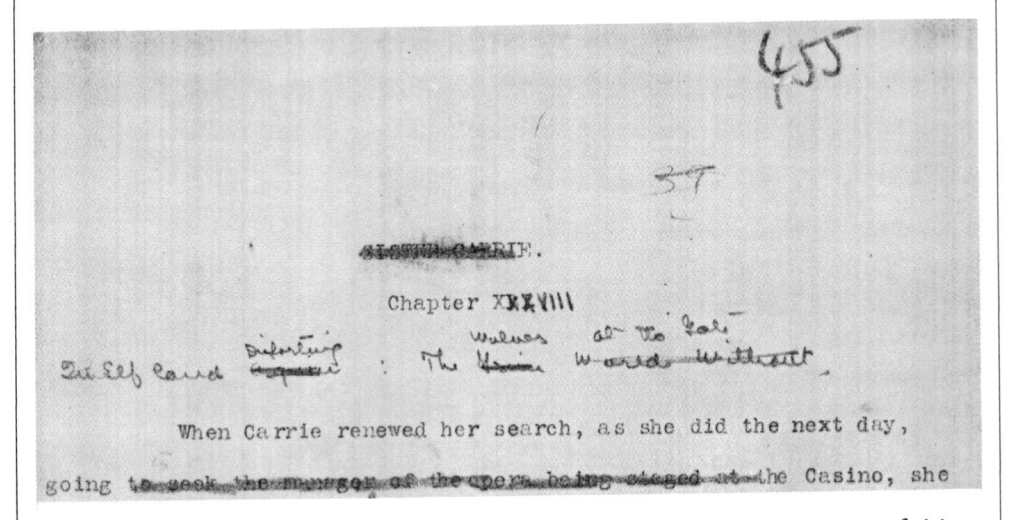

Detail from TS. 34: The chapter title and the initial cut are both by Henry.

Detail from TS. 455: Dreiser revises to emphasize the anapestic rhythm of this chapter title.

Dreiser and Henry also inserted chapter titles in the book, apparently at this time. Their reasons for adding these chapter titles are not known. The titles are metaphorical and poetic; most of them have a singsong rhythm when read aloud.

"It's a lie," he said, driven to a corner and knowing no other excuse.

"Lie, eh!" she said fiercely, but with returning reserve, "you may call it a lie if you want to, but I know."

"It's a lie, I tell you," he said in a low sharp voice. "You've searching around for some cheap accusation for months and now you think you have it. You think you'll spring something and get the upper hand. Well, I tell you, ~~~~~~, you can't. As long as I'm in this house I'm master of it and you nor anyone else ~~~~ dictate to me - do you hear?"

He crept towards her with a light in his eye that was ominous. Something in the woman's cool, cynical, upperhandish manner, as if she were already master, caused him to feel for the moment as if he could strangle her.

13

Detail from TS.260 showing galley markings by the compositor. The typed number "13" at the foot of the leaf is from an earlier pagination system; the typescript was prepared in chapters by Anna Mallon's typists, and each chapter was paginated separately.

Typesetting, Proofing, and Publication

The typescript went to the printer and was typeset. As the compositor finished each galley of type he marked the galley "take" on the typescript. By 22 September, ninety-four galleys had been set, bringing the compositor to the middle of chapter XXXI.

REMOVED TO
34 UNION SQUARE, EAST.
141-155 East 25th St., N. Y.

Sept. 22, 1900

Dear *Sir:*

     We are sending you by ~~this~~ *express*
~~mail~~ proofs of your book

"Sister Carrie"

as follows:

Galleys *50* to *94* inclusive.

Pages   to   inclusive.

     Please read and correct these and
return them to us at your earliest con-
venience, notifying us by the accom-
panying return postal of their despatch.

     Very truly yours,

DOUBLEDAY, & McCLURE CO.

DOUBLEDAY, PAGE & COMPANY.

This card was attached to one of the batches of
galleys sent to Dreiser.

Detail from MS.XIX.50: Dreiser's original sentence reads, "He was charmed by the pale face, made so by a touch of blue under the eyes, the lissome figure, draped in pearl gray, with a coiled string of imitation pearls at the throat." Dreiser means to stress the fact that Hurstwood is reacting to a false image of Carrie, heightened by makeup, costume jewelry, and the "make believe of the moment."

Detail from TS.224: Henry edited the sentence in typescript, removing the details that emphasized the artificiality of Carrie's appearance.

Detail from p. 205 of the 1900 text: The printer set *pearls* as *pears*, and the error went uncorrected in proof.

For the most part the typesetter did an accurate job, but there were occasional blunders and corruptions.

> "Isn't it just awful?" said Carrie, changing the drift of the conversation slightly. "Look at that man over there," and she began to laugh at a young man who had executed a comic fall.
>
> "How sheepish men look when they fall, don't they?" said Lola.
>
> "We'll have to take a coach to-night," answered Carrie absently.

Detail from TS.589: In typescript, Carrie laughs at the man who has slipped in the snow. This passage has important metaphorical overtones about "men who fall."

> " Isn't it just awful? " said Carrie, studying the winter's storm.
>
> " Look at that man over there," laughed Lola, who had caught sight of some one falling down. " How sheepish men look when they fall, don't they? "
>
> " We'll have to take a coach to-night," answered Carrie, absently.

Detail from p. 549 of the 1900 text. The passage was altered in proof to make Lola, Carrie's companion, laugh at the man. Carrie, as a result, seems less callous and more aloof.

Neither galleys nor page proofs survive for *Sister Carrie*, but by comparing the typescript to the published text one can discover what changes were introduced in proof. Some alterations appear to have been made by Dreiser, others by the publisher.

> "Well, then Wheeler," he said.   "I'll get the license the
> first thing in the morning."
>
>   The next day they were married by a Baptist minister, the
> first divine they found convenient.   ~~Hurstwood showed Carrie the city,~~

> " Well, then, Wheeler," he said.   " I'll get the li-
> cense this afternoon."
>   They were married by a Baptist minister, the first divine
> they found convenient.

Details from TS.348 and from p. 317 of the Doubleday, Page & Co. edition: In
typescript Carrie spends the first night in the Montreal hotel room with
Hurstwood, then marries him the next day. But the passage was changed in
proof, probably by someone at Doubleday, Page & Co. In the published book
they are now married the same afternoon they arrive in Montreal; then they
spend the night together, at least nominally wedded.

> You're the suckers that keep the poor people down - you bastards."
>
>   "May God starve ye yet," yelled an old Irish woman, who now
> threw   open a nearby window and stuck out her head.

> " Work, you blackguards," yelled a voice.   " Do the
> dirty work.   You're the suckers that keep the poor
> people down!"
>   " May God starve ye yet," yelled an old Irish woman,

Details from TS.506 and p. 466 of the 1900 text: The oath "you bastards" was
removed in proof.

SISTER CARRIE
THEODORE DREISER

The drab red casing of the Doubleday, Page & Co. edition. Dorothy Dudley, Dreiser's first biographer, called it an "assassin's binding."

Title page of the first edition, first impression.

Sister Carrie

By
Theodore Dreiser

NEW YORK
Doubleday, Page & Co.
1900

TO MY FRIEND

ARTHUR HENRY

WHOSE STEADFAST IDEALS AND SERENE DEVOTION TO TRUTH AND BEAUTY HAVE SERVED TO LIGHTEN THE METHOD AND STRENGTHEN THE PURPOSE OF THIS VOLUME.

The fulsome dedication to Henry
in the first impression.

Sister Carrie was published on 8 November 1900. The book was dedicated to Arthur Henry. Norris sent out 127 review copies and the notices were generally favorable, but the publisher did nothing else to promote the book and it was a commercial failure.

Intended for *Holiday Pages*

"O wad some power the giftie gi'e us
To see oursel's as ithers see us."

HENRY ROMEIKE,

110 Fifth Avenue,

Cable Address.
"ROMEIKE," NEW YORK.   **NEW YORK**.

The First Established and Most Complete
Newspaper Cutting Bureau in the World.

Cutting from *Literary Era*

Address of Paper PHILADELPHIA, PA.

Date

Sister Carrie. By THEODORE DREISER. Doubleday, Page & Co. $1.10. By mail, $1.22.

"Sister Carrie," a girl of eighteen, came to Chicago in the early 80's to look for work. She has longings for amusement and good clothes, and allows a handsome "drummer" to take care of her. Later she thinks herself married to the manager of a large drinking place. He takes her to New York, where she finally goes on the Casino stage. Her career is quiet and she never seems to realize her position. The author's theories of the longings in Carrie's nature that led her to despise work and need comfortable surroundings are unconventional. The temptations of working girls are described with utmost candor

George Seibel

in

PITTSBURG COMMERCIAL GAZETTE

Friday, December 28, 1900.

A NOVEL OF CITY LIFE.

"SISTER CARRIE." By Theodore Dreiser. New York: Doubleday, Page & Co. Pittsburgh: J. R. Weldin & Co. Price, $1.50.

If the function of the novel be to give lessons in the art of life, this book has not been born in vain. There are in it many lessons like the following:

"Well, if I were you," he said, looking at her rather genially, "I would try the department stores. They often need young women as clerks."

Was ever weighty truth enunciated so simply? Anyhow, Sister Carrie, who has come to Chicago to secure work, finally gets it at $4.50 per week. Life has more lessons for her to learn—lessons and temptations. Finally she gets upon the stage, in the chorus, at $12 per week. Here we have the difference between life and art. Carrie has learned her lessons well, and has now a diploma from the university of experience. If you doubt this, or if you doubt the novelist's depth of psychological insight into woman nature, here is a bit that will dissipate the doubt:

"I'll not give him the rest of my money," said Carrie. "I do enough. I am going to get me something to wear."

S. F. Chronicle

DEC 30 1900

A Feminine Type.

"Sister Carrie," by Theodore Dreiser, is a narrative of the career of an attractive and ambitious girl of 18, who visits her married sister in Chicago, and makes her way in the world by methods not always discreet or reputable. She finally marries a man under an assumed name—a defaulter—who removes to New York and has a hard struggle to keep the wolf from the door. The wife secures a position as chorus girl. She is showy and unembarrassed and attracts attention. As soon as she finds herself able to provide for her wants she leaves her husband with a curt note and a final farewell. Given a minor part in a society play, she makes a hit by accidentally working into it some new and taking stage business, and her name at once becomes a drawing card. Her salary is raised, and fame and fortune seem to be within her grasp. Meantime, her husband drifts downward. She refuses to meet or to assist him, and he commits suicide. She also turns her back upon others who had assisted her in her poverty, and discovers that she is thoroughly selfish, and has really never loved any one. And there the story leaves her. It is a long and complicated narrative, that is well handled and the chief character, though unlovely, is a distinct type. (New York: Doubleday, Page & Co.; price $1.50.)

"Sister Carrie" is a novel dealing with the sunny side of life in a manner which it is not too much to say is like that of Balzac. The writer shows insight into human nature and power of analysis and description. If this is, as some indications seem to show, his first book, and, if he is young, which nothing indicates, he ought to do some great work in the future. There is nothing more impressive in the year's novel-writing than the description of Hurstworth's last days, and death in New York. The book is rather long—556 pages—but it is full of action. One or two people of a moderate amount of honor would have strengthened the character group by contrast. All the people in the world are not hateful.

("Sister Carrie," by Theodore Dreiser. New York: Doubleday, Page & Co.)

In Halifax Consant, Dec 6, 1900.

Dreiser subscribed to a clipping service and pasted the reviews of *Sister Carrie* into a scrapbook.

DOUBLEDAY, PAGE & COMPANY
PUBLISHERS
34 UNION SQUARE, NEW YORK

FIRST REPORT.

NEW YORK, *Feb. 1,* 190*1*

Mr. Theodore Dreiser

DOUBLEDAY, PAGE & COMPANY SUBMIT THE FOLLOWING REPORT OF SALES

ON _*Sister Carrie*_ _____ RETAIL PRICE $ *150*

FROM PUBLICATION TO _*date.*_

COPIES RECEIVED FROM BINDERY		*558*	
ON HAND THIS DATE	*97*		
EDITOR'S COPIES	*127*	*224*	
COPIES SOLD		*334*	
EXEMPT FROM ROYALTY		*none*	
COPIES SUBJECT TO ROYALTY @ *15 cts*		*334*	*50 10*

Contra

Dec 7   Mdse
17   "
30   "

2 75
2 75
75   *5 25*

$44.85

Dreiser's disappointing first royalty report from Doubleday, Page & Co.

William Heinemann.

May 6, 1901.

Mr. Theodore Dreiser,
1599 East End Avenue,
New York City.

Dear Sir:

Our English agent reports
that Mr. Heinemann has practically concluded to issue "Sister Carrie" in his
Dollar Library, paying you a royalty
of 10%, provided you can condense the
first 200 pages of the book into 80
pages. He seems to consider this ab-
solutely essential, so if you feel that
this is impossible, let us know and we
will notify Mr. Roberts that he cannot
accept Mr. Heinemann's offer.

Very truly yours,

DOUBLEDAY, PAGE & CO.

Heinemann's offer to publish
a shortened version of *Sister Carrie*
was relayed to Dreiser by
Doubleday, Page & Co.

The British Edition

In May 1901 the London publisher William Heinemann offered, through Doubleday, Page & Co., to bring out an abridged edition of *Sister Carrie* in his "Dollar Library of American Fiction."

"Oh," he answered, in a very pleasing way and with an assumed air of mistake, "I thought you did."

Here was a type of the travelling canvasser for a manufacturing house—a class which at that time was first being dubbed by the slang of the day "drummers." He came within the meaning of a still newer term, which had sprung into general use among Americans in 1880, and which concisely expressed the thought of one whose dress or manners are calculated to elicit the admiration of susceptible young women—a "masher." His suit was of a striped and crossed pattern of brown wool, new at that time, but since become familiar as a business suit. The low crotch of the vest revealed a stiff shirt bosom of white and pink stripes. From his coat sleeves protruded a pair of linen cuffs of the same pattern, fastened with large, gold plate buttons, set with the common yellow agates known as "cat's-eyes." His fingers bore several rings—one, the ever-enduring heavy seal—and from his vest dangled a neat gold watch chain, from which was suspended the secret insignia of the Order of Elks. The whole suit was rather tight-fitting, and was finished off with heavy-soled tan shoes, highly polished, and the grey fedora hat. He was, for the order of intellect represented, attractive, and whatever he had to recommend him, you may be sure was not lost upon Carrie, in this, her first glance.

Lest this order of individual should permanently pass, let me put down some of the most striking characteristics of his most successful manner and method. Good clothes, of course, were the first essential, the things without which he was nothing. A strong physical nature, actuated by a keen desire for the feminine, was the next. A mind free of any consideration of the problems or forces of the world and actuated not by greed, but an insatiable love of variable pleasure. His method was

"I didn't say that," she said.

"Oh," he answered, in a very pleasing way and with an assumed air of mistake, "I thought you did."

Here was a type of the travelling canvasser for a manufacturing house—a class which at that time was first being dubbed by the slang of the day "drummers." His suit was of a striped and crossed pattern of brown wool, new at that time, but since become familiar as a business suit. The low crotch of the vest revealed a stiff shirt bosom of white and pink stripes. From his coat sleeves protruded a pair of linen cuffs of the same pattern, fastened with large gold-plate buttons, set with the common yellow agates known as "cat's-eyes." His fingers bore several rings—one, the ever-enduring heavy seal—and from his vest dangled a neat gold watch-chain, from which was suspended the secret insignia of the Order of Elks.

Lest this order of individual should permanently pass, let me put down some of the most striking characteristics of his most successful manner and method. Good clothes, of course, were the first essential, the things without which he was nothing. A strong physical nature, actuated by a keen desire for the feminine, was the next. A mind free of any consideration of the problems or forces of the world and actuated not by greed, but an insatiable love of variable pleasure. His method was always simple. Its principal element was daring, backed, of course, by an intense desire and admiration for the sex.

"Let's see," he went on, "I know quite a number of people in your town. Morgenroth the clothier and Gibson the dry goods man."

"Oh, do you?" she interrupted, aroused by memories of longings their show windows had cost her.

At last he had a clue to her interest, and followed it deftly. In a few minutes he had come about into her seat. He talked of sales of clothing, his travels, Chicago, and the amusements of that city.

"If you are going there, you will enjoy it immensely. Have you relatives?"

"I am going to visit my sister," she explained.

"You want to see Lincoln Park," he said, "and Michigan Boulevard. They are putting up great buildings there. It's a second New York—great. So much to see—theatres, crowds, fine houses—oh, you'll like that."

There was a little ache in her fancy of all he described.

An example of Henry's cutting. The unshaded areas in the American text (on the left) were excised for the British text (on the right).

Dreiser asked Henry to do the cutting for the Heinemann edition, and Henry did so, condensing the first 195 pages into about 90 pages. The artistic effect of Henry's abridgment was to move the reader more quickly through Carrie's story but to keep intact the sections dealing with Hurstwood. The Heinemann *Sister Carrie* is therefore Hurstwood's book, and his tragedy dominates the narrative.

" No," she said to herself, " he can't come here."

She asked Minnie for ink and paper, which were upon the mantel in the dining-room, and when the latter had gone to bed at ten, got out Drouet's card and wrote him.

" I cannot have you call on me here. You will have to wait until you hear from me again. My sister's place is so small."

She troubled herself over what else to put in the letter. She wanted to make some reference to their relations upon the train, but was too timid. She concluded by thanking him for his kindness in a crude way, then puzzled over the formality of signing her name, and finally decided upon the severe, winding up with a " Very truly," which she subsequently changed to " Sincerely." She sealed and addressed the letter, and going in the front room, the alcove of which contained her bed, drew the one small rocking-chair up to the open window, and sat looking out upon the night and streets in silent wonder. Finally, wearied by her own reflections, she began to grow dull in her chair, and feeling the need of sleep, arranged her clothing for the night and went to bed.

When she awoke at eight the next morning, Hanson had gone. Her sister was busy in the dining-room, which was also the sitting-room, sewing. She worked, after dressing, to arrange a little breakfast for herself, and then advised with Minnie as to which way to look. The latter had changed considerably since Carrie had seen her. She was now a thin, though rugged, woman of twenty-seven, with ideas of life coloured by her husband's, and fast hardening into narrower conceptions of pleasure and duty than had ever been hers in a thoroughly circumscribed youth. She had invited Carrie, not because she longed for her presence, but because the latter was dissatisfied at home, and could probably get work and pay her board here. She was pleased to see her in a way but reflected her hus-

and off he went, disappearing into the dark little bedroom off the hall, for the night.

" He works 'way down at the stock-yards," explained Minnie, " so he's got to get up at half-past five."

" What time do you get up to get breakfast ? " asked Carrie.

" At about twenty minutes of five."

Together they finished the labour of the day, Carrie washing the dishes while Minnie undressed the baby and put it to bed. Minnie's manner was one of trained industry, and Carrie could see that it was a steady round of toil with her.

She began to see that her relations with Drouet would have to be abandoned. He could not come here. She read from the manner of Hanson, in the subdued air of Minnie, and, indeed, the whole atmosphere of the flat, a settled opposition to anything save a conservative round of toil.

" No," she said to herself, " he can't come here."

After supper she asked Minnie for ink and paper, which were upon the mantel in the dining-room, and when the latter had gone to bed at ten, got out Drouet's card and wrote him.

" I cannot have you call on me here. You will have to wait until you hear from me again. My sister's place is so small."

When she awoke at eight the next morning, Hanson had gone. Her sister was busy in the dining-room, which was also the sitting-room, sewing. She worked, after dressing, to arrange a little breakfast for herself, and then advised with Minnie as to which way to look. The latter had changed considerably since Carrie had seen her. She was now a thin, though rugged, woman of twenty-seven, with ideas of life coloured by her husband's, and fast hardening into narrower conceptions of pleasure and duty than had ever been hers in a thoroughly circumscribed youth. She had invited Carrie, not because she longed for her presence, but because the latter was dissatisfied at home, and could probably get work and pay her board here. She was pleased to see her in a way, but reflected her husband's point of view in the matter of work. Anything was good enough so long as it paid—say, five dollars a week to begin with. A shop-girl was the destiny pre-figured for the newcomer. She would get in one of the great shops and do well enough until—well, until something happened. Neither of them knew exactly what. They did not figure on promotion. They did not exactly count on marriage. Things

Another example of Henry's cutting for the Heinemann edition.

SISTER CARRIE

BY

THEODORE DREISER

LONDON : WILLIAM HEINEMANN. 1901

The title page of the Heinemann edition.

The green cloth binding of
the Heinemann *Sister Carrie*.

DOUBLEDAY, PAGE & COMPANY
PUBLISHERS
34 UNION SQUARE, NEW YORK

FIRST REPORT.

NEW YORK. April 3th,   190 2

Theodore Dreiser, Esq.

DOUBLEDAY, PAGE & COMPANY SUBMIT THE FOLLOWING REPORT OF SALES

ON _____ "Sister Carrie" _____ RETAIL PRICE $__.96
        (Published by Wm. Heinemann, London)
FROM PUBLICATION TO. _____ January 1st, 1902,

COPIES RECEIVED FROM BINDERY .		2565	
ON HAND THIS DATE	1135		
EDITOR'S COPIES	219	1404	
COPIES SOLD		1161	
EXEMPT FROM ROYALTY		- -	
COPIES SUBJECT TO ROYALTY @ 7 1/2%		1161	$84 78

The royalty report on the Heinemann edition.

The British edition was widely promoted and sold relatively well.
Dreiser's royalties on the edition—paid to him through Doubleday,
Page & Co.—were not especially large, but they must have been grat-
ifying nonetheless.

Dreiser's contract with B. W. Dodge & Co. for a reissue of *Sister Carrie*. Dreiser put up $1,000 of his own money, signed over his royalties to Dodge, and agreed to work as Dodge's editorial director for stock in the firm rather than for wages.

Subsequent Textual History

After the publication of *Sister Carrie*, Dreiser went into a period of decline and eventually suffered a nervous collapse, partly as a result of his difficulties with the novel. He eventually recovered, however, and by 1906 had managed to acquire the unsold stock and the plates of *Sister Carrie*. In June 1907 Dreiser signed an agreement with B. W. Dodge & Co., a new publishing house, for a reissue of *Sister Carrie*. The terms of the contract were not especially advantageous to Dreiser, who had to take much of the financial risk himself, but he was anxious to see *Sister Carrie* republished and confident that the book would have a good sale.

82

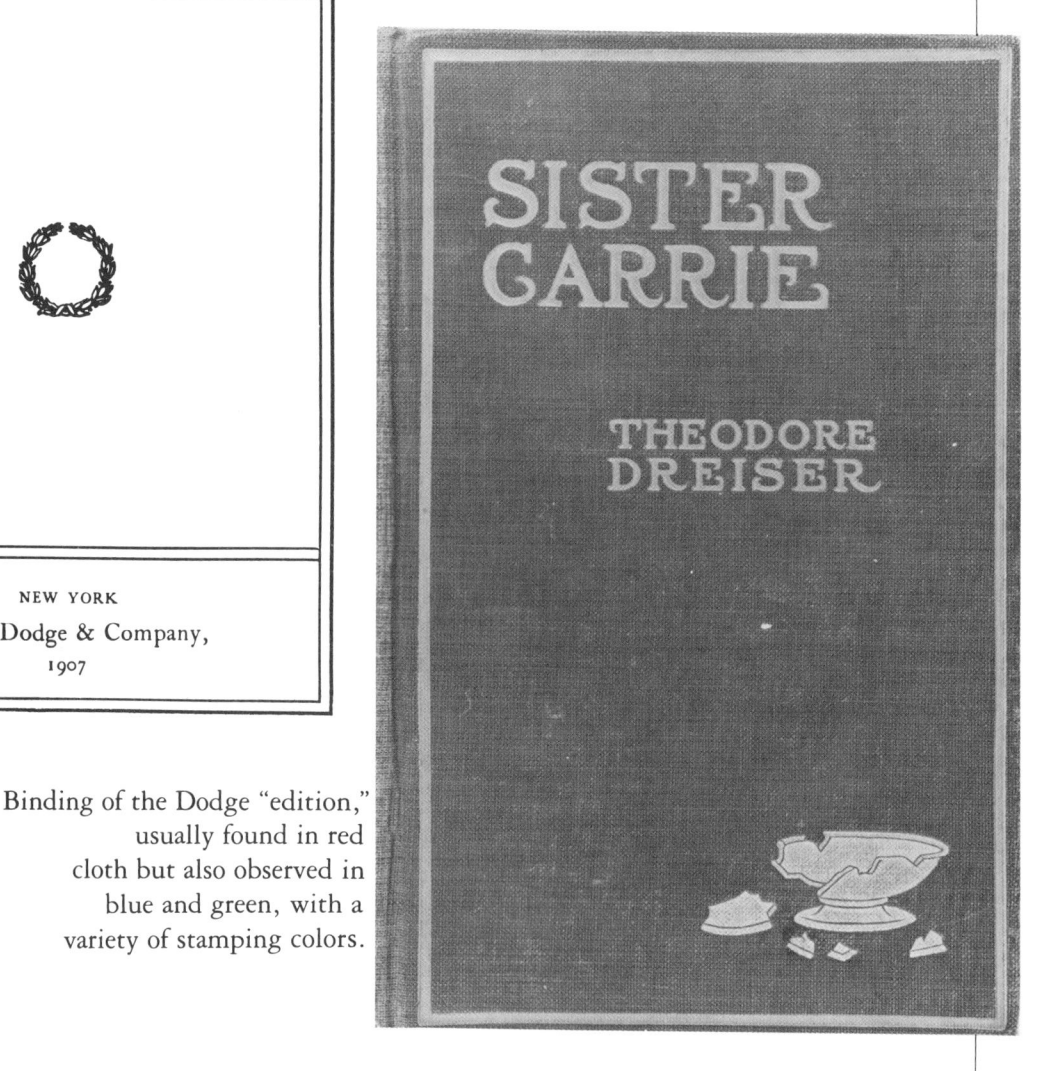

Sister Carrie

By
Theodore Dreiser

NEW YORK
B. W. Dodge & Company,
1907

Title page of the Dodge *Sister Carrie*.

Binding of the Dodge "edition," usually found in red cloth but also observed in blue and green, with a variety of stamping colors.

The B. W. Dodge "edition" appeared in May 1907 and sold some 8500 copies. For this text Dreiser removed the dedication to Arthur Henry, with whom he had fallen out. He also had the plagiarized passage from Ade altered in the plates. Dodge produced an attractive edition, with a colorful binding and a frontispiece showing Carrie on stage in her Quaker Maid costume.

The Ade passage in the 1900 text.

"Manager and Company realized she had made a Hit."—Page 4

The color frontispiece from
the Dodge *Sister Carrie*.

The revised version of the Ade passage, set by the printer and patched into the plates of *Sister Carrie* for the Dodge impression (and for all subsequent impressions from these plates).

It is further understood and agreed that HARPER & BROTHERS shall
have the privilege of publishing the AUTHOR'S next book upon the same terms
as are herein mentioned for "JENNIE GERHARDT"; and that the AUTHOR shall
deliver to HARPER & BROTHERS the plates of his book "SISTER CARRIE" without
charge to them, and they shall have the privilege of publishing a new
edition of the work upon the same terms as those herein mentioned for "JENNIE
GERHARDT".

HARPER & BROTHERS hereby agree to pay the AUTHOR upon the first publication of "JENNIE GERHARDT" the royalty which has been earned up to that time
by the sales of the said work under the terms of this agreement.

The said AUTHOR hereby authorizes and empowers his agent, Miss
F. M. Holly, 156 Fifth Avenue, New York City, to collect all sums of money
payable to the said AUTHOR under the terms of this agreement, and he declares
that her receipt shall be a good and valid discharge to all persons paying
such moneys to them.

Harper & Brothers.

Detail from p. 3 of Dreiser's contract with Harper & Bros. for publication of
Jennie Gerhardt.

Three years later in 1911, Dreiser finally completed his second novel,
Jennie Gerhardt, and published it with Harper & Bros. To keep *Sister
Carrie* on the market Dreiser had a clause added to the *Jennie* contract
for a second American republication of the novel. The Harper "edition" appeared in 1912 and enjoyed a long run of reprintings.

Two more editions of *Sister Carrie* appeared in Dreiser's lifetime, an unabridged text published by the British firm Constable in 1927 and an illustrated edition produced by the Limited Editions Club in 1939. Copyright on *Sister Carrie* passed into the public domain in 1956; since that year there have been some fourteen additional typesettings of the novel, of which the Pennsylvania edition is the most recent.

The Penguin American Library

THEODORE DREISER
SISTER CARRIE
THE UNEXPURGATED EDITION
INTRODUCTION BY ALFRED KAZIN

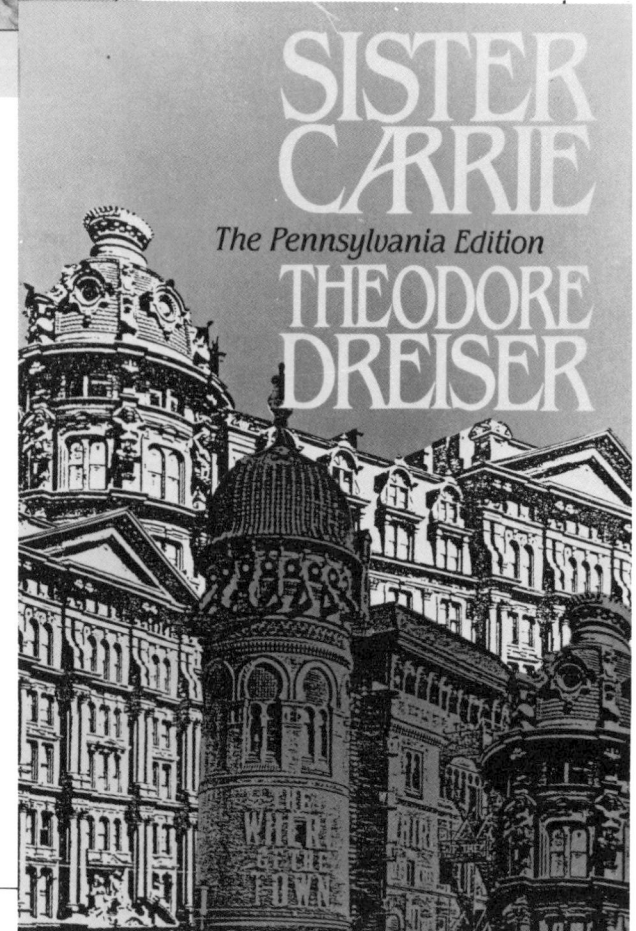